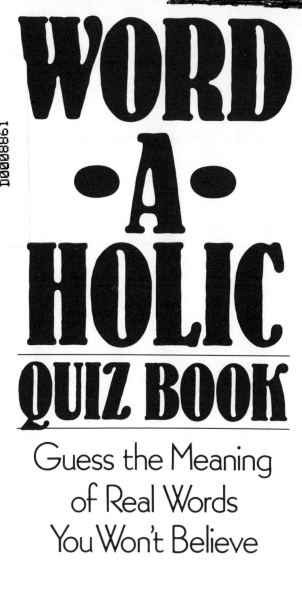

WORD ·A· HOLIC

QUIZ BOOK

Guess the Meaning
of Real Words
You Won't Believe

Carolyn Davidson

Sterling Publishing Co., Inc. New York

Edited by Jeanette Green

Library of Congress Cataloging-in-Publication Data
Davidson, Carolyn.
    Word-a-holic quiz book : guess the meaning of real words
you won't believe / by Carolyn Davidson.
        p.   cm.
    Includes index.
    ISBN 0-8069-0702-9
    1. Vocabulary—Problems, exercises, etc.   2. Questions and
answers.   3. Word games.   I. Title.
PE1449.D297W67   1995
428.1—dc20   95-9431
                                                            CIP

1   3   5   7   9   10   8   6   4   2

Published by Sterling Publishing Company, Inc.
387 Park Avenue South, New York, N.Y. 10016
© 1995 by Carolyn Davidson
Distributed in Canada by Sterling Publishing
% Canadian Manda Group, One Atlantic Avenue, Suite 105
Toronto, Ontario, Canada M6K 3E7
Distributed in Great Britain and Europe by Cassell PLC
Wellington House, 125 Strand, London WC2R 0BB, England
Distributed in Australia by Capricorn Link (Australia) Pty Ltd.
P.O. Box 6651, Baulkham Hills, Business Centre,
NSW 2153, Australia
Manufactured in the United States of America
All rights reserved

Sterling ISBN 0-8069-0702-9

DEDICATION

To my loving husband, Jim, and our two children, Mike and John, who mean all the world to me

ACKNOWLEDGMENTS

To Sheila Anne Barry and Sterling Publishing for their faith in my book; my editor, Jeanette Green, for ensuring that these words are in the "write" form; my dear friend Jan Winebrenner for her rare instincts, vision, and expertise; my friend Jay Gaines for his wit and wisdom; John Adcox for dotting my i's and crossing my t's; and my friend Micki Wright for her warmth and unique ability to deliver computer expertise in a soothing voice. (Don't wurry, Micki, I used spell ckek for the hole book.)

Contents

A Note from the Author

Welcome to the *Word-a-holic Quiz Book,* where I've collected some of the world's most incredible English words and their often surprising definitions. In these pages, you'll try to guess the meaning of real words you won't believe.

Did you know that the average English-speaking person uses the same 400 words 80 percent of the time? That means that the over 400,000 additional words in most standard English dictionaries often remain unused. Even well-read people and some lexicographers would have to do a little research to discover the meaning of many unusual words I've collected for this delightful vocabulary quiz book.

Each word used in this book has been carefully researched and can be found in either *Webster's Third New International Dictionary* (1986) or the compact edition of the *Oxford English Dictionary* (1971). These dictionary definitions have been slightly edited for readability and style. The false definitions used in this quiz, given side by side with the correct definitions, are, of course, the product of my imagination or those of fellow logophiles.

I first began collecting extraordinary words for my board game "You Said It!," created in the mid-1980s. When playing the game, often sparring on air with radio hosts and chatting with many people, I've gathered still more words to share with you. I'm convinced these amusing and intriguing words, like *cockarouse, willy-nilly, shilly-shally,* and *hugger-mugger,* will jump right off the page into your daily lives.

Although my chief aim is pure entertainment, you'll probably increase your vocabulary in the bargain. But be forewarned: I'll try to bluff, bamboozle, addle, obfuscate, outwit, and hornswoggle you in these pages, as you attempt to guess the real meaning of these unbelievable words. Since many of the words gathered here are uncommon or silly, and often sound preposterous, everyone can play the game, from eight-year-olds to octogenarians. You can enjoy the quiz alone or with a group. Everyone will have roughly equal footing and be able to make appropriate guesses.

It's time to turn the page, stimulate your *spizzerinctum* (will to win), stretch your *lexis* (vocabulary), and tickle your *olecranon* (funny bone). See, aren't you already having fun?

Carolyn Davidson

Directions

Each featured word, used in a sample sentence, is followed by three or more possible definitions—one genuine and two or more false, or bogus, definitions. The object is to choose the correct dictionary definition from among the decoys. Here's an example.

Bear with the *batalogist*.   *(ba-TOL-e-jist)*

a. a person who needlessly repeats the same thing
b. an inept batting instructor on a baseball team
c. a scientist who studies brambles.

The correct answer is "a."

For words tricky to pronounce, you'll find a pronunciation key in parentheses following the sample sentence, like that shown above for *batalogist*. The genuine definitions found in this book are the first given dictionary definitions for the selected words in *Webster's Third* or the *OED*.

Quiz words appear alphabetically with their correct definition in the Answer section at the back of this book. Question numbers and appropriate letter responses are given in parentheses (227-b) following each definition.

Let's Play Solitaire

In these pages you'll find words to enjoy. You can get into a gaming spirit and play alone, or choose a friend or two. The words await your defining mood. Deuces are wild and you'll surely encounter a joker or two.

1. Yep, those are *baggywrinkles*, all right.
(BAG-ee-RINK-l)

a. what plastic surgeons repair under the eyes
b. a popular Canadian snack similar to potato chips
c. a frayed rope on a ship

2. That pesky *pettifogger*! *(PET-ee-FOG-r)*

a. an airplane crop duster pilot
b. an Irish cop
c. a rascally attorney

3. Please pass the *pickelhaube*. *(PICK-el-haub)*

a. a relish tray
b. an unpleasant situation
c. a spiked helmet worn by German soldiers

4. So help me, she'll *shilly-shally* for hours.
(SHIL-ee-SHAL-ee)

a. drink Irish "hot toddies"
b. talk in a shrill voice
c. vacillate and be undecided

5. Ever flip a *liripoop*?   *(LEER-uh-poop)*

a. a person drawing suspicion
b. a tassel that hangs over a graduate's hat
c. counterfeit Italian money

6. A clueless *gumshoe*?

a. a person who puts her foot in her mouth
b. a detective
c. an incompetent cobbler

7. Practice the *paradiddle*.   *(PAIR-uh-DID-uhl)*

a. a military marching drumbeat
b. a parachute jump
c. a fiddle duet

8. Now, there's an *oxymoron* for you.
(OK-see-MOR-on)

a. a phrase that contradicts itself (i.e., a "quiet explosion")
b. eight politicians on one committee
c. an African bird

9. Did you read about the *hugger-mugger*?
(HUG-r-MUG-r)

a. an act of secrecy and concealment
b. a pickpocket
c. a family reunion

10. Let's *osculate*. *(AH-Skyu-layt)*

a. kiss
b. skip rope
c. drive fast

11. Where's the *cuckoo-button?*
(KOO-koo-BUT-in)

a. a prickly burr
b. a TV controller for channel hoppers
c. a snooze button on alarm clocks

12. He's lost his *aglets!* *(AG-lits)*

a. the metal coverings at the ends of shoelaces
b. marbles
c. agriculture newsletters

13. It sounds like *bumblekite* to me.
(BUM-buhl-kyt)

a. a blooper, a mistake
b. a belief that blackberries cause flatulence
c. the queen bee

14. So, find a *scaramouch*. *(SKAR-ah-moosh)*

a. a scarecrow in a field used to scare birds away
    from growing crops
b. a zombie triple feature
c. a stock character in the Italian commedia
    dell'arte

15. Bring in the *boodle*.   *(BOO-duhl)*

a.   estate and property
b.   tasty Chinese noodle casserole made with brown, unbleached flour
c.   a bundled baby

16. It's a *lalapalooza!*   *(LA-la-pu-LOO-zu)*

a.   an excellent person or thing; a humdinger
b.   Joe Palooka's sparring partner
c.   an Italian loafer (shoe)

17. Talk about a big *kerfuffle!*   *(ker-FUHF-uhl)*

a.   a Scottish foot soldier
b.   a commotion, fuss
c.   a woman's petticoat

18. Is that *kenspeckled*, or what?   *(KEN-spek-ld)*

a.   summer freckles
b.   Scottish word meaning conspicuous, having a distinct appearance
c.   species of trout found only in South America

19. He's a *quadragenarian*.
(QUAD-ra-jen-AR-ee-an)

a.   anyone between forty and fifty years old
b.   a mathematician who measures quadrangles
c.   a television actor who lasted just four seasons

20. Whoosh, a *williwaw!* *(WIL-ee-WAH)*

a. a sudden, violent gust of cold air
b. a Ferris wheel ride
c. a country and western dance

21. Did you catch the *taradiddle?*
(TER-ah-DID-l)

a. the fib
b. the joke
c. the innuendo

22. Great *googol!* *(GOO-gol)*

a. the figure "1" followed by a hundred zeros
b. stone sculptured figures on the outside of a building
c. delicious Indian licorice seeds

23. Who needs a *criticaster?* *(KRIT-i-KAS-tr)*

a. an inferior critic
b. an expensive salmon-fishing rod
c. a castor-oil plant

24. Have you read about the *splacknuck?*
(SPLAK-nuk)

a. a recovered Russian spacecraft
b. a wrestling hold
c. an unusual animal mentioned by Jonathan Swift in *Gulliver's Travels*

25. Who is a *cockarouse?*   (KOK-ah-ROWS)

a. a chicken farmer
b. a person of consequence among the American colonists
c. a cocker spaniel breeder

26. What are you, an *abbey-lubber?*
(AB-ee-LUB-r)

a. a fan of the "Dear Abby" newspaper column
b. a lazy monk
c. a wine salesman

27. Heck of a *hornswoggle!*   (HORN-swog-l)

a. a bamboozle, a hoax
b. a rodeo term meaning to wrestle a steer to the ground by grabbing its horns
c. a horn blast from a rude driver

28. Who is a *logomach?*   (LO-go-mak)

a. one who fights about words
b. one who cuts logs
c. one who designs corporate logos

29. Do you have a *niddy-noddy?*
(NID-ee-NOD-ee)

a. a bedtime drink, a hot toddy
b. any 7 A.M. college class
c. a hand reel for yarn

30. It's *wonky*, I tell you! *(WON-kee)*

a. a good deal
b. a brand name of a computer
c. unsteady, shaky

31. Is that a *nipperkin* on your lap?
(NIP-er-kin)

a. a container that holds a half-pint of hooch
b. a kissin' cousin
c. a small cocktail napkin

32. Are you a *philodox*, or what? *(FIL-e-doks)*

a. a native of Philadelphia, Pennsylvania
b. a person who just loves his own opinion
c. a medical conventioneer

33. Well, come *willy-nilly*! *(WIL-ee-NIL-ee)*

a. Willie Nelson's real name
b. a hyperactive child
c. "whether you like it or not"

34. A *dibble* is very effective. *(DIB-l)*

a. a Michael Jordan move
b. one of the 336 small depressions on a golf ball
c. a small hand instrument used to make holes in the ground for plants

35. A good *gazook?*   (ge-ZOOK)

a.   a graceful African antelope
b.   a guy
c.   an editor of a gazette

36. Indisputably a *wainwright!*   (WAYN-ryt)

a.   a word referring to the theme of John Wayne movies
b.   Orville and Wilbur's real surname
c.   one who builds and repairs wagons

37. Roaring b-b-b-b-*borborygmus!*
(BOR-bo-RIG-mus)

a.   a vain, macho-looking man, a living burst of sex appeal
b.   a growling intestine (time to eat!)
c.   the name of the monster in *The Thing* movie

38. I'm not a *pansophist,* but . . .
(PAN-suh-fist)

a.   a know-it-all
b.   a collector of Peter Pan memorabilia
c.   a hospital aide

39. *Griggles* galore!   (GRIG-ulz)

a.   small or inferior apples remaining on a tree after harvest
b.   uncontrollable, light laughter
c.   the pasta used to make spaghetti marinara

40. I love *dooteroomus*.   *(DOOT-r-OOM-us)*

a.   a cartoon character
b.   a do-gooder
c.   money

41. Look at this picture of a *belladonna*.
(BEL-ah-DON-ah)

a.   artistic carving over the doorway of antebellum
     homes
b.   a poisonous Eurasian plant having purplish red,
     bell-shaped flowers
c.   a female bellhop

42. You can almost picture the *farthingale* . . .
(FAR-thin-GAYL)

a.   a hooped petticoat worn in the 16th century
b.   a distant storm
c.   a European songbird

43. A *whippet* is a man's or woman's best friend.
(WHIP-it)

a.   a small dog
b.   someone sure to hit a home run
c.   small cooking utensil used to blend sauces

44. Get me a *balabosta!*   *(BAL-e-BOS-te)*

a.   an efficient Jewish housewife
b.   a bowl of hearty Romanian meat and potato stew
c.   a proprietor of a bowling alley

45. Who said there's no such thing as an *okapi*?
(o-KA-pee)

a. a giraffe-like animal with a short neck and black-and-white-striped upper legs
b. a pea and okra hybrid
c. a bird of the oklabar breed

46. He's a *quidnunc*, all right.   *(KWID-nunc)*

a. a busybody, newsmonger, gossip
b. Scottish term for "uncle"
c. an Aussie sweetheart

47. "Lights, camera, action. Uh-oh, there's a *blizzard head* in view."   *(BLIZ-ard head)*

a. a ski resort portable outhouse
b. a cold beer
c. a woman television performer with hair so blonde that special lighting is required to prevent a flare or halo from appearing on screen

48. Listen to the *yaffle*.   *(YAF-uhl)*

a. a green woodpecker that makes a laughing sound
b. a yacht's steam whistle
c. a rifle having a short barrel and large bore

49. This seems like a *whiffle* to me! *(WIF-el)*

a. something light or insignificant, a trifle
b. an inhaler used by people with a respiratory problem
c. a stingray

50. Pardon the *pother!* *(PO-thr)*

a. old-fashioned shaving soap
b. a noisy disturbance, bustle
c. a favorite old sweater

51. Hey, are you a *quaddle*, or what? *(KWAHD-dl)*

a. a person who grumbles
b. any foursome (as in golf)
c. the catcher in baseball

52. My *pantofle*, please! *(pan-TOHF-ul)*

a. a bedroom slipper
b. the hot mixture for taffy before it is removed from heat
c. woman's drawers, bloomers

53. *Celerity*, my foot! *(se-LER-u-tee)*

a. a low-profile personality, not a celebrity
b. the state of not having a spouse; single life
c. swiftness, speed

54. A *kickshaw* would be perfect.   *(KICK-shaw)*

a.   a fancy dish in cookery
b.   a motorized rickshaw
c.   a sled popular in Scandinavia

55. A *graphospasm* has set in.
(GRAF-o-SPAS-m)

a.   a writer's cramp
b.   a computer virus
c.   a form of chalk engraving

56. I've never worn a *hug-me-tight*.

a.   a woman's short, close-fitting bed jacket
b.   a hula skirt
c.   a medieval hooded cloak

57. Do you have *horripilation?*
(HOR-i-pul-A-shun)

a.   goosebumps
b.   a literary compilation of horror books
c.   a bad memory

58. Jumping *jumbuck!*   *(JUM-buk)*

a.   a sheep native to Australia
b.   your first dollar made
c.   a person in charge of jumping (as for parachute troops)

59. *Lagniappe* **will brighten your day.**
(lahn-YAP)

a. a plate of plain pasta
b. a late arrival
c. a small gift given a customer by a merchant at the time of a purchase

60. *Nuddle* **your way through it.**   *(NUD-l)*

a. to stagger through a project or assignment
b. to push with the nose often close to the ground; to grovel.
c. a hockey term—when players gather for a conference on the ice in a huddle

61. Find the *singlet.*   *(SIN-glet)*

a. the matching sock the dryer "swallows"
b. an undershirt or athletic jersey
c. a woman's undergarment to keep her waist cinched

62. She's a *scapegrace.*   *(SKAP-gras)*

a. an agnostic
b. a reckless, unprincipled person
c. a guest at an inn who, according to Saxon law, after having stayed for three nights, was considered one of the family

63. That dirty *dipsy doodle*.   *(DIP-sy-DOO-dl)*

a. a fondue pot
b. a metal rod for indicating depth of oil
c. a bewildering plunge and lag by turns (e.g., "the dipsy doodle price of rice")

64. Beware of the *honeycreeper!*

a. a schnook you fell in love with though you knew better
b. a small brightly colored oscine bird of the Coerebridge family found in tropical and subtropical America
c. a sweet perennial herb

65. Oh, for a little *oenotherapy!*
(EEN-o-therapy)

a. the use of wine for therapeutic purposes
b. the use of herbs for therapeutic purposes
c. the use of massage for therapeutic purposes

66. Call me *callipygian*.   *(KAL-ah-PIJ-ee-an)*

a. having a shapely bottom (buttocks)
b. having shapely fingers
c. having high cheekbones

67. That's my *yokefellow*.

a. a comedian
b. a close associate or companion; a partner in marriage
c. a country bumpkin; country folk

68. Have you met an *uxorious* husband?
(uk-SOR-ee-us)

a. unfaithful
b. a Charles Atlas bodybuilder type
c. doting on, with excessive fondness for, and often submissive to, a wife

69. Just can't kick the *katzenjammer*.
(KAT-sen-JAM-r)

a. a cat
b. pajama habit
c. hangover (the nausea, headache, and debility following drunkenness)

70. *Singultus!*   *(sing-ULT-us)*

a. hiccups
b. sneezing
c. coughing

71. Aw, look at the *flews*.

a. the large chaps (hanging upper lips) of a deep-mouthed hound, like a bloodhound
b. an unclipped boxer ear
c. the act of a dog turning around and around until it finds a comfortable place to lie down

72. Clearly a *jabiru*.   *(JAB-uh-roo)*

a. a large stork of tropical America
b. that deft insult that gets you where it hurts
c. close living quarters

73. Watch for the *gardyloo*.   *(GARD-ee-loo)*

a. a female guard
b. a brownish gray European warbler
c. a warning shout in Scotland when it was customary to throw household slops from upstairs windows: "Attention to the water!"

74. Save the *klapmatch*.   *(KLAP-match)*

a. a female seal
b. a two-handed card game
c. a long, ornate fireplace match

75. What's a *gillflirt*?   *(GILL-flirt)*

a. a giddy or shameless girl
b. a relentlessly flirting man
c. a fisherman

76. *Give me gill-go-by-the-ground.*

a. a merry-go-round
b. a round of hot toddies
c. ground ivy

77. "*Ladykin, ladykin,* fly away home!"
(LAD-ee-kin)

a. a distant relative, such as a great aunt
b. a little lady, sometimes used as an endearment
c. a female folksinger

78. It's *holus-bobus*.

a. the chant of a crystal ball gazer
b. all in a lump, all together
c. sunspots

79. What's a *quahog*?   *(KWO-hog)*

a. a trough from which hogs eat
b. a four-wheeled tractor
c. a thick-shelled American clam

80. The *cockshut* crept up on me.   *(COK-shut)*

a. evening twilight
b. paparazzi
c. crocodile

81. Yo, a *younker*!   *(YON-kr)*

a. a legal term referring to a debt
b. a person from Yonkers, New York
c. a young man, child, youngster

82. Begin your morning with an *aubade*.
(o-BAHD)

a. a German highway
b. a song greeting the dawn
c. a cereal made of oats, raisins, and nuts

83. Let's sit by the *inglenook.* *(IN-gel-nook)*

a. a corner by the fire
b. a cabinet for knickknacks
c. the opening to an Eskimo's igloo

84. Care to *canoodle?* *(ka-NOO-dl)*

a. to cuddle amorously
b. to paddle a canoe
c. to use a can opener

85. It could be a *cattalo.* *(KAT-l-oh)*

a. a chute through which cows are herded onto trucks
b. a hybrid of the American buffalo and the domestic cow
c. the sound of contented cattle, a lowing sound

86. Watch the *woolly bear.*

a. a rhythmic animal dance among North American Indians imitating the bear
b. a bearded seal
c. a very large caterpillar

87. Come to think of it, it's a *contrabass.*
(KON-trah-bays)

a. largest instrument of the viol family
b. game warden
c. hard rock music aficionado

88. Be careful when you're on *kittly-benders!*
(KIT-lee-BEN-drs)

a. go-carts
b. in-line skates
c. thin, bending ice

89. Hear the *jingbang?*   *(JING-bang)*

a. Chinese fireworks display
b. crowd, company
c. Salvation Army volunteer's Christmas bell, used to attract attention and donations during the holiday season

90. What's a *tinker's damn?*

a. a small dam
b. a young Yankee
c. something absolutely worthless

91. Remember the *Tin Lizzie?*

a. a nickname for the Model T Ford automobile
b. the first can opener
c. a loin guard with decorative inlays on medieval armor

92. A *penster* weighs his words carefully.
(PEN-ster)

a. an agricultural auctioneer
b. a prison warden
c. a writer

93. Would you be a *woodmonger?*
(WOOD-mon-ger)

a. a dealer in wood, timber merchant
b. a chair-warmer, do-nothing
c. a neighbor who puts up a fence to make a statement to you

94. *Coxcomb* covers all.   *(COX-coom)*

a. a woman who never tires of primping
b. a woman with a slight mustache
c. a jester's cap worn by a professional fool

95. Bring your own *chicha!*   *(CHEE-chah)*

a. a South and Central American beer made from fermented maize
b. a tenderfoot in Alaska
c. a cylindrical brimless cap of Arab origin, often having a tassel on the crown

96. Come over for *calipash.*   *(KAL-e-pash)*

a. the fatty, gelatinous, dull green substance found under the upper shell of a turtle that's esteemed as a delicacy
b. a covered-dish supper
c. a milk chocolate, marshmallow, and nut candy

97. Ask an *agrostographer*.   *(AG-ro-STOG-ra-fr)*

a. a writer whose subject is grass
b. a writer whose subject is agriculture
c. a writer whose subject is group dance that includes mime of planting and harvesting, related to crop maturation

98. Divvy out the *dandiprat*.   *(DAND-ee-prat)*

a. practical jokes
b. satirical lampoons and literary mockery
c. English silver coin of the 16th century, probably worth twopence

99. She is a *prickmedainty*.
(PRIK-mee-DAYN-tee)

a. an unfaithful spouse
b. affectedly nice; goody-goody
c. a female practicing Chinese acupuncture, using special needles to cure disease

100. A pep talk from the *poo-bah*.   *(POO-bah)*

a. a minister of the cloth
b. someone holding many public or private offices
c. a school cheerleader; a person who calls for and directs organized cheering

101. Take a peek at the *pook*.

a.   heaps or small stacks of hay or grain
b.   a picture book
c.   a small cave

102. Ahh, my sweet *amoret*.

a.   a demitasse of fully roasted amaretto-flavored coffee
b.   a semiprecious stone
c.   a sweetheart; an amorous girl

103. Light up that *loco foco!*   *(LO-ko-FO-ko)*

a.   miniature train with all the lights and whistles
b.   match or cigar developed during the 19th century that's capable of being ignited by friction on any hard, dry, rough surface
c.   a locomotive engineer's quarters

104. She wants to *snoozle*.

a.   to cuddle, snuggle
b.   to eat sugar-coated noodles
c.   to blow her nose with a handkerchief

105. That sharp *snippersnapper* got me!

a.   lawn tool used on hedges and bushes
b.   fingernail clipper
c.   whippersnapper

106. The *howdie* hung out her shingle.
(HOW-dee)

a. midwife
b. cowgirl
c. church greeter

107. He's got the *kinkcough*.   *(KINK-koff)*

a. that early morning cough
b. cough drop
c. whooping cough

108. Catch sight of the *checkerbelly*.

a. the chassis of a Checker cab
b. an extinct species of whale
c. a white-fronted goose

109. No doubt, a *niddle-noodle*.

a. an unstable nodding head
b. a pasta chef
c. a golf club

110. What is a *billywix*?   *(BIL-lee-wiks)*

a. the belt holster for a policeman's billy club
b. the last part of a burned-out candlewick
c. a tawny owl

111. Give the boy a *baksheesh*.   *(BAK-sheesh)*

a. a spanking
b. a tip; gratuity
c. a chair to sit on

112. He is in *kidcote*.   *(KID-coht)*

a. jail
b. a lamb petting zoo
c. an elementary school coatroom

113. It isn't worth the *diddle daddle!*

a. money
b. piece of paper it's written on
c. fuss

114. So, what is a *smicket*?

a. chocolate nut candy bar
b. slightly stifled laugh
c. woman's smock (English)

115. A *vamper* was hung by the chimney with care.

a. a stocking
b. a note to Santa
c. a cookie for Rudolph

116. Save the *bungtowns*.   *(BUNG-townz)*

a. whales
b. hometowns
c. copper tokens resembling English halfpennies that circulated in the U.S. in the 18th and 19th centuries

117. With a breeze come *diddledees*.

a. fallen pine needles
b. those little pancake drippings on an outdoor grill
c. colored sticks used in popular preschool game "Diddledeed" (can be blown over easily)

118. Winnie, what is the *pooh-pooh theory?*

a. a theory that language originated in interjections which gradually acquired meaning
b. a potty-training theory, made popular by Dr. Spock
c. a theory that negative thinking dominates most people

119. Does the *dingdong theory* ring a bell?

a. a theory that says you need to stay fit and healthy until you're dead
b. a theory that says if you lie around, eat Ding Dongs, and watch soap operas, you'll gain weight
c. a theory that language originated from a natural correspondence between objects of sense perception and the vocal noises which were part of early humans' reaction to them (whew!)

120. Zero in on the *Zingaro*.   *(DZING-ar-o)*

a. the Italian name for Gypsy, or Rom
b. an insult or put-down
c. the citadel in the port Zanzibar

121. The *flicker-a-flacket* finally fizzled out.

a. an 18th century oil lamp
b. a person who has a difficult time resisting flicking lint off another person's shoulder
c. a representation of the sound made by something flapping

122. Call it *cacography*.   *(ka-KOG-re-fee)*

a. elegant writing or penmanship
b. bad writing; bad handwriting
c. charting of hurricanes

123. *Auspice* is the answer.   *(O-spes)*

a. a program of economic controls aimed at reducing current consumption
b. the use of spices in cooking
c. observation, especially of the flight and feeding of birds, intended to discover a sign of the future

124. Can't top a *belltopper*.

a. a church steeple
b. the small top layer of an ornate wedding cake
c. a tall silk hat (Australian)

125. Beware of the *bee louse*.

a. a minute wingless fly parasitic on honeybees
b. the bee in a hive that cleans the queen bee
c. a common form of head lice

126. *Bumfuzzled again?*   *(bum-FUZ-ld)*

a. champagne that doesn't fizz or pop a cork
b. confused, perplexed, flustered
c. wrapped in a warm muffler about the neck

127. What is *fimble*?

a. a game of catching candy from burning brandy
b. a finger thimble used in sewing for a left-handed person
c. the male hemp plant that produces a weaker and shorter fiber than the female plant

128. Just what is a *justaucorps*?
(ZHOOST-o-cor)

a. a man's close-fitting, knee-length garment; a body coat
b. a body—yes, a *dead* body
c. a dress uniform for a U.S. Marine

129. *Niddle* now!

a. a Swedish surgeon calling for his needle in surgery
b. the cap or end of a flashlight battery
c. to move quickly

130. Notice the *niddicock.*

a.   a cocktail waitress
b.   a cocker spaniel breeder
c.   a fool, a ninny

131. Here's a bona fide *bobadill.*   *(BOB-uh-dil)*

a.   a small dill pickle
b.   a bobsled contestant in the Alaskan Iditarod Trail
     Sled Dog Race
c.   a cowardly braggart

132. Bring back the *bunny hug!*

a.   an American ballroom dance in ragtime rhythm,
     popular in the early 20th century, in which a
     couple holds each other closely
b.   a fast hug
c.   the old pregnancy test in which the rabbit died if
     the lady's results were positive

133. You could be bogged down in *burgoo.*
(BER-gu)

a.   another name for swamp grass
b.   a mud hole near a lake or river
c.   a thick oatmeal gruel used chiefly by seamen

134. I daresay that's called a *dingbat*.

a. the type of bat usually found in belfry or bell
    towers
b. a typographical ornament (as a bullet or star)
    used typically to call attention to an opening sen-
    tence
c. an Australian wolf-bat that lives in trees

135. Bring out the *ballhooter*.   *(BOL-hoot-r)*

a. another name for the batboy on a baseball team
b. a machine used to inflate footballs, basketballs,
    and soccer balls
c. a logger who rolls logs down slopes too steep for
    teams of horses

136. It's *zooty!*   *(ZOO-tee)*

a. a word used by chimney sweeps to describe a
    dirty fireplace
b. the vest of a zoot suit in the 1940s
c. extreme or flashy in manner or style

137. "Excuse me, what time is it?"
"It's about *pretty-by-night*."

a. noon
b. four o'clock
c. midnight

138. Get a *gamp*.   *(GAMP)*

a. slang for umbrella
b. an electrical measurement, as in 4-gamp fuse
c. the name for a protector of Sinbad

139. The poor *pea goose*.

a. a poor simpleton; ninny
b. a pillow stuffing made with peas in the 19th century by farmers
c. a small, distant relative of the Canada goose

140. "Oh, do you see the *draggle-tail?*"

a. a common plant in swamps; looks like a cat's tail
b. a scared puppy
c. a woman who lets her skirt trail along the ground

141. Everything is *hotsy-totsy* now.
(HOT-see-TOT-see)

a. too hot to handle
b. comfortably stable or secure
c. all downhill now—things are going well

142. Keep track of the *kittle cattle*.

a. small, wild Australian cattle
b. cattle deemed too skinny for market
c. a group of people difficult to manage and inclined to be capricious

143. Find that *twit-twat.*

a. a bug in a computer program
b. the switch or handle that controls the speed of a diesel engine
c. a house sparrow

144. Pick out the *pennywinkle.*

a. those small grooves on the edge of a penny
b. a periwinkle
c. a cheap corsage

145. Is there even a *paradoctor* in the house?

a. a doctor who reaches isolated areas by parachute
b. a doctor specializing in paralysis of legs
c. a retired doctor who works only part-time

146. That's a flaming *flamdoodle.*   *(flam-DUD-l)*

a. a dessert on which brandy is poured and lit with a match
b. someone who draws cartoons or doodles, especially while taking notes
c. a line of pretentious nonsense

147. It's *fair dinkum!*

a. unquestionably good or genuine; excellent—often used as a general expression of approval (Australian)
b. a baseball term: a hit that goes for extra bases
c. advertising posters for a state or local fair

148. I figure it's *fairy butter*.

a. morning dew on the grass
b. blue-green algae, forming gelatinous sheets or pellets
c. another name for cream cheese

149. A *hubble-bubble* can be trouble!

a. a water pipe
b. a glitch in the Hubble Telescope
c. the froth that forms in rain gutters and drains, seen when it's raining

150. A *huckaback* may be too rough to handle!
(HUK-u-BAK)

a. an Australian hitchhiker
b. the stem on which huckleberries grow
c. a tough, durable type of cotton

151. Too many *jimjams!*

a. nightgowns
b. delirium tremens; also, overwrought from excess or fear
c. small, wild flowering plants indigenous to South America

152. He's the *jack-in-office*.

a. a jack-of-all-trades; a person who fixes all that needs fixing
b. a gofer; the runner
c. an insolent fellow in authority

153. Just a *jack-a-dandy*.

a. a jack-o'-lantern made from a green pumpkin
b. a little, foppish, impertinent fellow
c. a jack-high straight in poker

154. Don't chew your *claro*.   (*KLA-ro*)

a. the mouthpiece for a clarinet
b. a gelatin-based dessert
c. a light-colored, generally mild cigar

155. She's a *chuffy* one.   (*CHUF-fee*)

a. one who wears a chef's hat
b. fat, chubby
c. a type of cat

156. He's so *bellicose*, he's blue in the face.
(*BEL-e-kos*)

a. short of breath
b. warlike, aggressive, combative
c. cold

157. He's loose from the *calaboose*.
(*KAL-ah-boos*)

a. the last car on a train
b. nickname for telephone booth
c. jail

158. Come to think of it, it's a *cowfish*.

a. an old cowboy term used to describe the poor cowboy chosen to hunt for stray cows: "He went fishing for cows."
b. a wide-bottomed sailboat popular on northern lakes
c. any of various small cetaceans, such as the grampus and some species of porpoise and dolphin

159. It's just *jiggery-pokery*, I tell you.

a. humbug, nonsense (British)
b. another term for a night out with the boys for drinking and playing poker
c. a foolish, silly dance

160. Sounds like *sine die* to me.
(syn-nay-dy-ay)

a. a trigonometry function
b. fate
c. indefinitely; without any future date designated to resume business

161. A simple *siffleur*.   *(seef-FLER)*

a. a type of French flour used in baking
b. a whistler
c. a small flower grown in France

162. Watch out for the *spanker boom.*

a. a small paddle used by 19th century teachers to discipline students
b. a fishing bonanza—when a ship's spankers are running
c. the boom for a spanker on a ship

163. A small *bittock.*

a. the birdie in badminton
b. a little bit (Scottish)
c. the hinge part of a horse's bit and bridle

164. Back away from the *blue devils.*

a. low spirits, melancholy
b. pranksters
c. fiery, hot sauces made from Mexican blue peppers

165. *Tarantism* can take its toll.
(TAR-en-TIZ-m)

a. a student studying the influence of the Torah; study of the Torah
b. a dancing mania caused by the bite of a tarantula
c. a disease of the thorax

166. *Quark!*   *(KWARK)*

a. the biblical name for Noah's ark
b. one million to the 10th power
c. croak

167. It's a *quiddity*, my dear!   (*KWID-it-ee*)

a. a hairsplitting distinction
b. a small bank, much like a piggy bank, used by English children to save money
c. the handle on an arrow quiver used by bow-and-arrow enthusiasts

168. In and out the *inquiline*.   (*INK-wil-yn*)

a. medicine or drug used in treatment of insomnia
b. the holder for a quill pen
c. an animal that lives habitually in the nest or abode of some other species

169. It seems like a *swell mob* to me.

a. the accumulated or consistent ocean swells flowing to a beach
b. a political clique composed of members of the winning political party
c. a group of criminals who dress fashionably and act with seeming respectability

170. Of course, the *Oregon boot!*

a. a heavy iron shackle attached to the ankle and foot of a prisoner to prevent escape
b. special boot with cleats used by lumberjacks
c. a geographic region in Oregon, famous for its leather manufacturing

171. We'll meet at the *wayzgoose*.   *(WAYZ-gus)*

a. a printer's annual outing or entertainment
b. a children's petting zoo
c. a German hotel for travelers

172. Pick up a *pottle*.   *(POT-l)*

a. the handle on a pot
b. the handle on a canoe paddle
c. a liquid or dry measure equal to a half-gallon

173. The poor *Popocrat* sat next to the fire.
(POP-e-krat)

a. a Democrat supporting Populist policies in the last decade of the 19th century, usually used disparagingly
b. kernels remaining after corn has popped; unpopped corn, named for Colonel Popocrat's ineffectual American Civil War battles
c. a small firecracker

174. That's a run-of-the-mill *rudesby*.
(ROODS-bee)

a. the code of ethical conduct associated with the game of rugby
b. a pallor of the skin after too much sun and wind exposure
c. an uncivil, turbulent person

175. Use *pilliwinks* with precision.
(PILL-eh-winks)

a.   an old instrument of torture for the thumbs and fingers

b.   an instrument used by a pharmacist to measure grams of pills

c.   a device to measure the amount the average person blinks in his sleep at night

176. The pill takers are grateful to the *pill masser*.

a.   a hypochondriac

b.   a pill passer; a registered nurse

c.   a machine that mixes ingredients for pills

177. There's nothing like a good *pillowbeer*.
(PILL-o-beer)

a.   a cold beer

b.   a pillowcase

c.   a pillow fight

178. She's just a *pigwidgeon*.   *(pig-WIDG-en)*

a.   an insignificant or simple person

b.   a person who collects porcelain porcine memorabilia

c.   a person who wears her hair tied in a pigtail

179. You can swear by the *quarson*.
(KWAR-sen)

a. a clergyman who also holds the position of squire in his parish
b. the son of a squire
c. a reliable son

180. Sink or swim with a *kelpie*. *(KELP-ee)*

a. an Australian inner tube made of kelp
b. a vegetable pie made from sea kelp
c. a doll that floats

181. All in the family are with the *neffy*.
(NEF-ee)

a. variation of "nephew"
b. the maiden name of a married woman
c. the wife of one's nephew

182. It's *picotee* time. *(PIK-eh-tee)*

a. a pretty colored golf tee
b. a time to become particularly angry
c. a flower (as carnation, tulip, rose) having one basic color with a margin of another color

183. As a matter of fact, they're *melophagus*.
(mel-OFF-uh-gus)

a. a genus of six-legged spiders
b. a genus of wingless flies
c. a genus of winged flies

184. Like it's *lip-deep!*

a. plunged in to the lips (no deeper than the lips)
b. a type of facial cream
c. to move the lips in synchronization with recorded sound, as lyrics to a tune

185. Not the *naricorn.*   *(NAR-i-korn)*

a. a person who behaves in a mawkish or unsophisticated manner
b. a horny covering protecting the nostrils in certain birds
c. a social gathering for husking corn

186. Indisputably *napoo!*   *(na-POO)*

a. British slang used to indicate that something is finished, incapacitated, dead, all gone, or nonexistent, or that the answer is "no"
b. nap time
c. an infant's diaper

187. There's rarely a good night's sleep for a *noctambulist.*   *(nok-TAM-byu-list)*

a. a painter of night scenes
b. a musical composer intending to suggest or evoke thoughts and feelings of night
c. one who walks at night, especially in his sleep

188. Oh, to *oscitate*.   *(OS-i-tayt)*

a. to yawn
b. to kiss
c. to stretch

189. Put up the *pelmatogram*.
(pel-MAT-e-gram)

a. a telegram carried by foot
b. a pell-mell, jumbled telegram
c. an impression of the sole of the foot

190. Who or what is a *king plank*?

a. the center plank of a wooden deck
b. a practical jokester
c. the president of Planned Parenthood

191. Gee whiz, what's a *gee-throw*?

a. a game of horseshoes
b. a sloppy, journalistic mode of writing
c. a strong wooden lever with a curved metal point used to break out logging sleds

192. Head out for a *hoddy-doddy*.

a. someone who does not surf but spends time at surfing beaches pretending to be a surfer
b. a garden snail
c. a person who carries a trough over the shoulders for transporting loads, such as bricks

193. A half-baked *hoddypoll.*

a. a fumbling, inept person
b. a brick
c. a cookie

194. She's a *moll-buzzer.*

a. a person who walks a shopping mall for exercise
b. a person whose job is to vacuum the mall
c. a pickpocket whose victims are women

195. Me, a *molly-coddle?*   *(MOL-ee-COD-l)*

a. a person who studies molecular beams
b. a pampered darling; a spineless weakling
c. a person who just loves to cuddle

196. Yes, I think *yeti* really exists.   *(YET-ee)*

a. an artificial language using geometric forms to represent words that was created for communication between chimpanzees and humans
b. the Abominable Snowman
c. a sea monster in Norwegian legends

197. I bow to the *bowwow theory*.

a. a theory that a bow tie will make a good first impression
b. a theory that bowlegged cowboys are still desirable
c. a theory that language originated in imitations of natural sounds, such as those of birds, dogs, or thunder

198. Let's run the *Nantucket sleighride*.

a. a New England airline
b. a run in a whaling boat to a harpooned whale
c. a snowmobile manufactured in Nantucket

199. I'll have *pease porridge*, if you please!

a. an ailment of the inner ear
b. pea soup
c. a bouquet of wild flowers

200. Alexander Hamilton was once an *aide-de-camp*. *(ayd-di-KAMP)*

a. an immigrant to America
b. a politician challenged to a duel
c. a military aide

201. The *aileron* roll has me all shook up.
(AYL-er-on)

a. a roller coaster ride
b. a flight maneuver in which an airplane rotates about its longitudinal axis through a full 360 degrees (by means of ailerons) without altering its flight path
c. a four-wheeled carriage with two seats and a standing top

202. Bring a *kef* to the party.

a. a state of dreamy tranquility
b. a creamy drink made of fermented cow's milk
c. a small cask or barrel

203. *Kiss-me-over-the-garden-gate!*

a. a plant
b. a large kingfisher, native to Australia, with a call that resembles kissing sounds
c. a male salmon in spawning season

204. *Kiss-me-quick.*

a. an assassin bug that inflicts a painful bite on a sleeping person, often on the lips
b. mouth-to-mouth resuscitation
c. a small bonnet worn off the face, especially in the latter half of the 19th century

205. Count it all *koh-i-noor*.   *(KO-ee-nor)*

a. something thought to be the best of its kind, especially an unusually large and valuable diamond
b. a native Korean
c. Korean currency

206. Where is the *kissing gate*?

a. a kissing booth
b. ticketed entrance to a drive-in theatre
c. a gate swinging in a V-shaped enclosure that allows only one person to pass at a time

207. *He's betwixt and betwattled!*   *(be-TWAT-ld)*

a. tattled upon
b. addled, confused
c. between

208. *Beturbaned is better.*   *(be-TUR-band)*

a. the right to dig peat or turf on someone else's ground in Turkey
b. an aircraft in which a turbofan is used
c. one who is wearing a turban

209. It's *infradig*.   *(IN-freh-dig)*

a. in the frig
b. beneath one's dignity
c. in the hopper; being considered

210. A *bib nozzle* is only a big deal if you don't have one.

a. a handkerchief
b. the bent up portion of a baby's bib that catches the "mess"
c. a bent-down nozzle of a faucet, often threaded for attachment of a hose

211. "Pop" goes the *popinjay*.   *(POP-in-jay)*

a. a tab that can be pulled up or off to make an opening
b. a parrot
c. a pop fly ball in baseball

212. Bring to a *bibliophile*.   *(BIB-lee-o-fyl)*

a. a lover of books, especially those with beautiful or rare formats
b. a person whose sole job is to file papers
c. a person who loves to study the Bible

213. A *bibliotaph* always keeps extras.
(BIB-lee-o-taf)

a. a tippler; drinker
b. a person who hides or hoards books
c. a collector of Bibles

214. Why does he *nid-nod?*

a. to nod repeatedly from drowsiness
b. to wear a small feather in a hat
c. to play marbles in a bent-over style

215. A *polyglot* is never at a loss for words.
(POL-ee-glot)

a. a parrot
b. a person who speaks or writes several languages
c. a person who has more than one wife

216. *Echolalia* can be annoying!   *(eko-LAL-ee-a)*

a. pig Latin
b. the ability of an animal, such as a bat or dolphin, to orient itself by the reflection of the sound that it produces
c. the often pathological repetition of what is said by other people, as if echoing them

Go for Gustation

If you're dining out with friends and they ask for *goonch* (fried catfish) to go with the *plonk* (cheap wine), you'll know that you're dining with true *logolepts* (word lovers).

Many of the words in this chapter sound like something edible or something you'd find in the kitchen. Both false and real definitions may relate to food. I threw together this word feast the way I cook, improvising on a recipe, sprinkling a little parsley here and a little lemon there, and having a great time. I added a fourth definition for each word, just for good measure. So, attack this banquet of words with relish.

217. There's a *pannikin* in the kitchen.
(PAN-i-kin)

a. a rookie dishwasher
b. a panic—total pandemonium
c. a small cup or pan, often of tin
d. a table waiter

218. Let me show you what to do with an *inky-cap*.
(INK-ee-kap)

a. a jar opener
b. a mushroom
c. an electric can opener
d. the fruit of an inkberry

219. Go for the *gustation!*   *(gu-STAY-shun)*

a. a Swedish smorgasbord
b. a Norwegian smorgasbord
c. the sensation of tasting
d. the sensation of smelling

220. An *oleaster* with oomph is hard to find.
(OH-lee-AS-ter)

a. a wild olive tree
b. a Swedish cookie
c. a good Easter bread
d. a Norwegian casserole

221. You have a *bathbun* in the kitchen?

a. a chef's hat
b. a plant of the genus *exanthem*
c. a round bun made of sweet yeast dough, containing eggs, butter, and currants
d. an unfired brick used to polish metals

222. *Gorp* is good for you.

a. a healthy mixture of dried fruit, nuts, and seeds
b. a whole-milk cheese made in the Netherlands
c. a beef stew made with onion, paprika, and caraway seeds
d. a fruit with a hard rind

223. Pass the *honeypot*.

a. a hollowed-out honeydew melon
b. a receptacle for storing honey
c. money saved in a receptacle for the honeymoon
d. the name for the nest of a wild honeybee

224. I can never resist a *napfkuchen*.
(napf-KOOGH-en)

a. napkin
b. soft leather chair
c. semisweet cake (German)
d. the last cookie left on the plate, which everyone is too polite to take

225. Use a spoon; it's *bonnyclabber*.
(BON-ee-KLAB-r)

a. baby food
b. thick, sour milk
c. covered candy, shaped like a boomerang, with a center of sugar to which fruits and nuts are sometimes added
d. appetizer served before a seafood dinner

226. Choose *gimcrackery* if you wish.

a. chocolate sprinkles
b. the sweetened lime juice added to cooling drinks
c. a collection of flimsy doodads, knickknacks, or trifles
d. rye crackers

227. We're having savory *badderlocks* for supper.
(BAD-r-loks)

a. smoked salmon
b. large brownish black seaweed often eaten as a vegetable in Europe
c. seaman's stew made of meat, vegetables, and hardtack
d. tripe sausages

228. Beware of the *lickerish* appetite.
(LIK-r-ish)

a. slightly inebriated
b. a black toffee-like candy made from the root of the licorice plant
c. fond of fine food, eager to taste or enjoy
d. a Russian bread

229. Barbecue the *gillaroo*.   *(gill-uh-ROO)*

a. Irish trout
b. garlic bread
c. New Orleans shrimp
d. frogs' legs

230. Turn on (if you can) to *toad-in-the-hole meat.*

a. another name for a doughnut
b. a crawdad or crayfish
c. meat (as sausage) cooked in batter, usually by baking
d. uncooked frogs' legs

231. Take it easy when making *tipsy pudding*.

a. original name for eggs Benedict, prepared for restaurant customers with a bad hangover
b. tapioca made with brandy
c. stale sponge cake soaked in wine, especially sherry, and served with custard
d. several-layered Jell-O

232. Pick the *paranut*.   *(PA-ra-nut)*

a. Brazil nut
b. seed of a pear
c. parboiled peanut
d. pine nut

233. Everybody loves a *love apple*.

a. apricot
b. oyster
c. tomato
d. baked apple

234. Make a hit with *milk punch*.

a. the liquid from a coconut
b. another name for eggnog
c. strawberry-flavored milk drink
d. a mixed drink of alcoholic liquor, milk, and sugar

235. The _poonac_ is a piece of cake.   *(PU-nac)*

a. coconut cake
b. parking space for vehicles at a tarmac restaurant
c. a puma's den, where these animals feed their young
d. dock for people in canoes to picnic at

236. Keep an eye on the _kielbasa._
(keel-BAH-sah)

a. a Norwegian campsite
b. a Polish apartment complex
c. a type of wood found in Poland from which bass fiddles are made
d. uncooked smoked sausage

237. Beware of the _biscuit shooter!_

a. a kitchen utensil used in making biscuits to ensure uniform size
b. a cook or waiter, especially in a camp or on a ranch
c. the original name for the famous BB air rifles
d. a famous racehorse

238. I'm bent upon having a *Banbury tart*.

a. a waitress of loose morals; a floozy
b. banana bread
c. an often triangular tart with a fruit filling, especially of raisins, from Banbury, England
d. a popover

239. What is a *nipa*?

a. slang from the 1940s and 1950s for a Japanese child
b. a very short nap
c. an hors d'oeuvre made with salmon
d. an alcoholic beverage made from the fermented sap of an Australian palm

240. Now, what good is a *nodding onion*?

a. an absent-minded nutrition professor
b. a widely distributed North American bulbous herb with white to deep rose flowers, also called a wild onion
c. an onion with small stems growing on its side
d. a type of cooking measurement—a dash of chopped onion in a recipe

241. This is no doubt a *nodding catchfly*.

a. a perennial European sticky herb
b. the action of a horse waving its tail to chase away flies
c. an easy out in baseball
d. a fishing lure used to catch trout

242. Just try the *jelly roll*.

a. a sequence of piano notes, popularized by Jelly Roll Morton
b. any jelly doughnut
c. a thin sheet of sponge cake spread with jelly and rolled up while hot
d. a ceremonious wiggle that gelatin does when you set it down rather hard on the counter

243. It's time for a toast with *tim-whiskey*.

a. whiskey
b. near-beer
c. milk
d. lemonade spiked with whiskey

244. Is *dog cabbage* on the menu?

a. asparagus in chicory leaves
b. an untrimmed head of cabbage
c. lettuce
d. a fleshy southern European herb often eaten as a potherb

245. Make one's mouth water with *Jim Hill mustard*.

a. tumble mustard named after James J. Hill
b. a tart red currant sauce
c. a pine nut and orange flour water sauce
d. a carrot and onion glaze consisting of salt, sugar, butter, and stock

246. *Jigger pump,* I'm gonna . . . pump you up.

a. a waitress's working shoe (pumps)
b. a small spritzer gadget that pumps out Christmas cookies
c. a pump used to make flavored Sno-Kones
d. a pump to force beer into vats

247. Justify *jackalegs*—if you can.

a. frogs' legs served in brandy sauce
b. fried rabbit
c. a large clasp knife (Scottish)
d. Alaskan snow crab legs and claws

248. Suck up to the *belly robber!*

a. a cook; steward
b. a corset or girdle
c. a diet food such as rice cakes
d. an elastic waistband

249. Hard as a *quahog.*   (KO-hog)

a. a four-motorcycle caravan of Harleys
b. a thick-shelled American clam
c. a wild Arkansas razorback hog
d. a software program for hog farmers

250. Pig out on *pigs in blankets*.

a. oysters, chicken livers, or other choice morsels wrapped in thin slices of bacon, fastened with skewers, and broiled or sauteed
b. feta cheese kabobs
c. ham quiches
d. roasted pigs at a Hawaiian buffet

251. Please pass the *pishpash*.

a. a pickle mixture; relish
b. a punch mixture
c. a German word for a pâté
d. a rice broth containing bits of meat

252. Cook up some *kumara*.   *(KUM-era)*

a. a kale salad
b. a plum and apple kuchen
c. a sweet potato (New Zealand)
d. kumquats in cognac

253. What is a *nehu*?   *(NE-hu)*

a. a small Hawaiian anchovy much used for bait
b. a hot Oriental nut canapé
c. a caterer from the Netherlands
d. a new potato casserole

254. Oh, for some *oopak!*   *(U-pak)*

a. oysters with eggplant
b. any of several black teas grown in Hupeh province in China
c. packages for Brie
d. orange peel stuffing packed inside turkeys in Japan

255. Here's a *rarebit* for you.

a. Welsh rabbit; melted and often seasoned cheese sometimes mixed with ale or beer and poured over toasted bread or crackers
b. a South Pacific swordfish
c. a tiny morsel
d. rare meat; too pink

256. Savor some *shepherd's pie.*

a. a lamb dish
b. stuffed chops
c. a savory mixture of leftover meat baked in a crust of mashed potatoes
d. a pie made with sugarcane, rhubarb, and strawberries

257. Break the ice with *baked Alaska*.

a. a hot buttered rum punch
b. also called snowy flip; a recipe of whipped cream, milk, and brandy
c. a dessert consisting of cake topped with ice cream covered with meringue and quickly browned in an oven
d. a whipped potato casserole

258. Let's partake of the *buttercup squash*.

a. a crushed pat of butter
b. a cup of buttered squash
c. a turban squash with flesh resembling a sweet potato in flavor
d. a crowded social function

259. Consider the *cock-a-leekie*.

a. a leaky tureen
b. a soup made of chicken boiled with leeks
c. a cracked cocktail glass
d. a weather vane on top of a chicken restaurant roof

260. Yikes—*cock ale!*

a. ale fermented with fruits, spices, and the jelly or mincemeat of a boiled cock
b. ale made by a cook with a big ego
c. cock-and-bull story, told while drinking cock ale
d. ale for pilots to drink in the cockpit

261. Guzzle the *gazoz*.   *(guh-ZOZ)*

a.   grapefruit and white wine punch (Scandinavian)
b.   German word for wine
c.   a carbonated nonalcoholic drink
d.   a glass of spring water

262. Ho, ho, ho, a *hoecake!*

a.   a cake made by you know who
b.   a small cake made of cornmeal, water, and salt, so named from its being baked on the blade of a hoe
c.   the cake you put out for Santa
d.   a carrot cake

263. Sip the *slumgullion* slowly.
(slum-GUL-yen)

a.   a drink made popular at slumber parties
b.   a sloppily presented beverage
c.   an insipid drink, such as weak tea or coffee
d.   a drink made popular by winos

264. Stay clear of *squirting cucumber*.

a.   a Mediterranean plant having oblong fruit that bursts from the peduncle when ripe and forcibly ejects its seeds
b.   slang for ketchup bottle
c.   a lemon
d.   a coconut

265. A *samlet* is a small fry.

a. Spam
b. a small shrimp-and-steak combo
c. a young salmon
d. a mini Salisbury steak

266. Soak up a little *sippet*.

a. a small snack
b. a pet's supper
c. just a sip
d. a small bit or piece of toast soaked in milk or broth

267. Celebrate with *syllabub*.   *(SIL-ah-bub)*

a. a television gourmet cook, such as Graham Kerr
b. slang for champagne
c. a drink or dessert made by curdling milk or cream with wine or other acid
d. another name for tipsy fruit fool

268. Pawn off the *ponhaws*.

a. a dish of leftovers, scrapple
b. small undesirable shrimps
c. crawfish
d. lobster tail shell

269. We have *hippocras* at "happy hour" today!
(HIP-po-kras)

a. a hippopotamus and lettuce sandwich
b. the meal served after physicians complete the Hippocratic oath
c. a spice-flavored wine
d. hot toddies

Calling All Sports Fans

How's your *spizzerinctum* (will to win)? Grab a cold drink and pull up a comfortable armchair for "Monday-morning quarterback" play. In this chapter all kinds of sporting words—jargon or not—are fair game. If you're already in the pros, some of these may seem like rookie words. You may hit home runs every time you swing, while other words may become real squeakers for you. But you won't be stopped by a referee if you try to steal a few bases by sneaking a peek at answers in the back. Remember, a few of these words are off the wall, perhaps not sporting at all. But I trust you'll find them.

Use this chapter for goodwill games with friends, if you choose, but then again, a little one-upmanship with fellow players probably won't draw whistles and hoots from the crowd or manic hand gestures from the referee. Allow this chapter to put words in your mouth when you go to the ballpark (or simply take the book along). Whether you're playing in the All Stars or the minor leagues, you know it's three strikes and you're out. But, hey, you can always have a rematch with a whole new set of curve balls, fast balls, and fancy words. Batter up. Let's go. Play ball!

270. Mix it up with a *mashie niblick.*

a. an old golf club, also called a six iron
b. a wrestling match; a period of wrestling
c. the practice of tattooing the inside of a race-
    horse's lip as a means of positive identification

271. Ahoy! *Dockwalloper!*   (dok-WOL-o-pr)

a. driver of a small locomotive designed to work in
    close quarters around a waterfront
b. a loafer about docks who picks up casual employ-
    ment
c. a dock builder

272. What's a *fipple?*   (FI-pl)

a. a football term for a poorly thrown ball
b. a flexible tapering fishing pole of split bamboo
c. a grooved plug in the end of a whistle

273. How's your *spizzerinctum?*
(SPIZ-r-INK-tem)

a. the will to succeed; vim, energy, ambition
b. side-to-side movement in skiing
c. term for a pitcher's windup in baseball

274. Are you searching for a *spelunker?*
(spe-LUNK-r)

a. someone who explores caves
b. a mountain climber
c. a snow skier

275. *View halloo!*

a. a shout uttered by a hunter on seeing a fox break cover
b. a victory lap done at the end of an auto race for all to see the winner
c. a lifeguard's call for all swimmers to come within his view at once

276. Go for a *gedunk*.   *(GE-denk)*

a. a professional basketball dunk made famous by Michael Jordan
b. a specific dive in the Summer Olympics
c. something (as a sundae) sold at a soda fountain or snack bar

277. Catch the *kittenball*.

a. jai alai ball
b. badminton birdie
c. softball

278. Bye bye *birdie*.

a. to shoot a hole in golf in one stroke under par
b. an English hockey puck
c. the feathered end of an arrow

279. Let's close up shop and get with the *cuttyhunk*.

a. the barrel in which scotch whiskey is aged
b. a hand-laid twisted linen fishing line suitable for deep-sea sport fishing
c. an English male model

280. We could be blazing through with a *ballahoo*.
(BAL-ah-hu)

a. song from the Broadway musical *South Pacific*
b. a political speech
c. a schooner of Bermuda and the West Indies with its foremast raking forward and its main staff aft

281. So, he's a *stumblebum* is he?

a. a punch-drunk, clumsy, or inept boxer
b. slang for an archaeologist
c. a person who plays a stringed musical instrument

282. I was punched out by the *palooka*.
(pe-LUK-ah)

a. a pig-lifting contestant
b. a Polish ski jumper
c. an inexperienced or incompetent boxer

283. Watch for a knockout by a *knuckle-duster*.

a. racquet ball racquet
b. brass knuckles
c. boxing glove

284. Go for the *gopher ball*.

a. a hole-in-one in golf
b. a term for a good billiard shot
c. a pitched ball hit for extra bases, specifically one hit for a home run

285. Make a hit with a *Minié ball*.

a. a term for a very small Ping-Pong ball.
b. a rifle bullet having a cylindrical body, conical head, and hollow base, much used in the mid-19th century
c. a small dinner dance; often written on invitations as "black-tie Minié ball"

286. Gee whiz! A *guitarfish*.

a. any of several viviparous rays of the family rhino-batidae, somewhat resembling a guitar in outline when viewed from above
b. brand name for a top-of-the-line guitar
c. a ball thrown in bowling that seems to roll in the shape of a guitar and which ends in the gutter

287. He has a way with *halieutics*.
(hal-ee-YU-tiks)

a. the art of fishing
b. the art of hoisting or lowering a sail in sailing
c. playing a hole or a round in golf in match play in the same number of strokes as one's opponent

288. Did he *foozle* again?

a. play unskillfully; to bungle
b. take part in a face-off in ice-hockey
c. give a fake to an opponent

Time to Cock-a-hoop and Party

This chapter is perfect for word-a-holics at after-work confabs, birthday celebrations, dinner parties, family gatherings, and holiday or other get-togethers. You may even find that you've delayed that dinner, ceremony, or gift-opening for one more round of word play. You can use these quiz words to play with as many as thirty or even sixty people—simply break up into teams. Try men against women or even adults against the kids. It's a great party ice-breaker for people who don't know each other well. Each teammate should try to convince his opponents that he alone provides the correct meaning of a chosen word. But just one team member tells the truth while others give false definitions. The opposing team determines who holds the actual definition shown on these pages. *Argy-bargy* (lively debate) will ensue. Who is telling the truth, and who is fibbing? This party game invites a humorous race for winning points for your team (or you), while all participants increase their vocabularies as well.

As the game intensifies, you'll learn to detect the personality quirks of would-be malaprops. You may notice your opposition becoming shifty-eyed, trying to contain an uncontrollable smile or silly grin, tapping a busy foot, or looking away. That's how you'll know who's bluffing. If you're right, you win a point. If you're wrong, well, you've been bamboozled. So, get ready for another round. Let the party begin!

289. Much ado about *ballyhoo*.   *(BAL-ee-hoo)*

a. a game of jacks
b. a song from the musical *South Pacific*
c. an attention-getting demonstration or talk, as by
    a barker

290. It's time to *cock-a-hoop!*   *(KOK-uh-HOOP)*

a. to live extravagantly
b. to put on a plastic or metal hoop for twirling
    about the body
c. to pierce the ears for earrings

291. *Crambo*, anyone?   *(KRAM-boh)*

a. a game in which one player gives a word or line
    of a verse that's matched in rhyme by other play-
    ers
b. a card game
c. spin the bottle; a kissing game

292. Let the *bumble-puppy* begin.
(BUM-bel-PUP-ee)

a. a square dance
b. an old game resembling bagatelle, but played out-
    doors with marbles
c. a singles mixer

293. Let's *schmooze* a while.   *(SHMOOZ)*

a. chat
b. nap
c. kiss

294. Look at all the *heliophiles* flocking to the beach.   *(HEL-ee-o-fyls)*

a. people attracted to sunlight
b. seagulls
c. parasailers

295. Don't invite a *swillbowl* to your swell party. *(SWILL-bol)*

a. a drunkard
b. a swooner; someone in love
c. an unfaithful spouse

296. Toast with a *toby*.

a. the life of the party; a party animal
b. a prepared short speech
c. a small jug, pitcher, or mug generally used for ale and shaped like a stout man with a cocked hat

297. He's *blotto*!   *(BLOT-toh)*

a. winning at backgammon
b. playing psychologist
c. completely drunk

298. The celebration is incomplete without *blithemeat.*

a.   music prepared for a feast to celebrate the birth of a child
b.   food prepared for a feast to celebrate the birth of a child (Scottish)
c.   flowers prepared for a feast to celebrate the birth of a child

299. Avoid blowing the *bubblet.*

a.   a small hot-tub party
b.   the main ingredient in bubble gum
c.   a small bubble

300. A *jack-pudding buffoon* will perk up the party.

a.   a clown
b.   the Dutch equivalent of a Mexican piñata
c.   an English dessert made with custard and jack-berries, served in a large flower-shaped bowl called a buffoon

301. Just where is the *jinglet?*   *(JING-let)*

a.   the clasp that holds jingles to a bracelet
b.   the musician in a symphony orchestra who plays bells
c.   the bell clapper of a sleigh bell

302. It's just a *jokelet*.

a.   a little joke
b.   a jestbook
c.   a joker

303. Bring on the "*beer and skittles*."

a.   an English television show
b.   drink and play; easy-going enjoyment
c.   a Scottish phrase meaning "bringing home the bacon," or supporting one's family

304. It's time for the *beanfest!*

a.   a small Boston festival that celebrates the popularity of Boston baked beans
b.   a bean sorter in a bean cannery
c.   a noisy good time (British)

305. What is a *jingo ring*?

a.   the third ring around Saturn
b.   a singing game in which children join hands and dance around one child in the center
c.   the ring inserted into a cow's nose used to lead a cow or bull around

306. Carry the *climax basket*.

a.   a small, oblong veneer basket with rounded ends
b.   a mountaineer's pack holding a climbing axe
c.   a basket for carrying balloon and weather instruments

307. Try cool *coolamon*.   *(KUL-e-man)*

a. an Australian vessel of bark or wood that resembles a basin and is used for carrying and holding water
b. teen talk
c. a shower (Jamaican)

308. Here's a *prosit* for you.   *(PRO-zit)*

a. large overstuffed chair common in the 18th century
b. bit of professional advice
c. a toast used to wish good health, especially before drinking

309. Point out the *pennyprick*.

a. an old game of aiming at a penny
b. manager of a penny arcade
c. a small-scale bet in poker

310. Enjoy *kiss-in-the-ring*.

a. a ceremonial gesture, to kiss the ring as a sign of brotherhood in Christian liturgies
b. the game drop-the-handkerchief, in which the pursuing player may kiss the player he catches
c. a Swedish wedding tradition where the bride and groom kiss each other's ring before putting it on

Around the World
in Many Words

A Dallas radio show host asked me the meaning of one of his favorite words, *shunpiker*. I hadn't heard the word before but provided a bluff answer that turned out to be the word's genuine definition. A shunpiker avoids highways, driving on slower, more relaxing, and scenic back roads. I like to think of him as taking the road less traveled. He shuns tollways and turnpikes, and you'd never see him on the German superhighway, the Autobahn.

In this chapter, we'll meander off the main road, exploring with lexical levity (the joy of *lex?*) countries around the world. You could pack some of these words with other *needments* in your suitcase and head for your car, bus, train, or plane. Or you could take an imaginary journey. Just turn the page. Buckle up, lower the top of your convertible, smell the fresh air, and explore the backroads of Scotland, Peru, India, Tibet, Australia, and Poland with me. Here are some uncommon words you may encounter in your travels.

311. Watch that *zap flap?*

a. an airplane wing flap
b. a Spanish flamenco dance
c. an Australian bird

312. Do you want to do the *wonga wonga* in the garden?   *(WON-gah-WON-gah)*

a. an Australian woody vine with loose panicles of yellowish white flowers
b. a slow Japanese folk dance
c. a sinuous Polynesian dance performed by men and women

313. *Wiki wiki* to all.   *(WEE-kee-WEE-kee)*

a. a Hawaiian welcome; a newcomers' party
b. a Hawaiian farewell party
c. a Hawaiian adverb meaning quickly, fast

314. Take the *tonga*.

a. a bicycle built for two
b. a light two-wheeled vehicle for two or four people drawn by one horse, common in India
c. a small Japanese cap

315. That's *kaka* talk!   *(KAH-kah)*

a. New Zealand parrot that talks and mimics well
b. Slavic parrot that talks and mimics well
c. Croatian parrot that talks and mimics well

316. A chattering *titi*.   *(TEE-tee)*

a. a loquacious Irish manservant
b. a South American monkey
c. a talkative golfer

317. Remember your first *simoleon?*
(suh-MOH-lee-yun)

a. dollar
b. floor made from wood products, similar to linoleum
c. copycat game, as in Simon Says

318. The elusive *dragoman.*   *(DRAG-uh-mun)*

a. what every wife tries to take to the shopping mall
b. an interpreter, chiefly of Arabic, Turkish, or Persian, employed as official interpreter by an embassy or as a guide by tourists
c. a male dragonfly

319. Swat that *zimb!*   *(ZIM)*

a. a large two-winged fly native to Abyssinia
b. a moth from Monaco
c. a mosquito from Michigan

320. A *zarf,* anyone?

a. a cup-shaped holder for a hot coffee cup used in the Levant, usually of metal and of ornamental design
b. a German beer mug
c. an oyster fork

321. A terrific *tzut!*   *(TSOOT)*

a. a set of garments consisting of a long, loose coat and trousers worn in the Middle East
b. a Tibetan terrier
c. a brightly patterned square of cotton used by Guatemalans, especially as a head cover

322. Take me to a *ziggurat.*   *(ZIG-e-rat)*

a. an ancient Babylonian temple
b. a zillionaire
c. a sewing machine factory

323. I smell a *perwitsky.*   *(pur-WIT-skee)*

a. a Scottish tobacco pipe
b. a red, white, and black European tiger weasel
c. a Polish meat pie

324. Would you like a *beenamarriage?*
(BEEN-ah-MAR-ij)

a. a marriage in Australia in which the wife has little authority
b. a marriage in the United States in which the children have all the authority
c. a marriage in parts of India and Ceylon in which the husband enters the wife's kinship group and has little authority in the household

325. Dance to the sounds of the *doodlesack?*
(DOO-dl-sak)

a.   an accordion
b.   a bagpipe
c.   a fiddle

326. *Pip-pip!*   *(PIP-PIP)*

a.   "Party on!"
b.   "So what?" "Who cares?" (British)
c.   "So long!" "Good-bye!" (British)

327. *Farkleberry* is my favorite!
(FAR-kel-BER-ee)

a.   a small scone
b.   a Scottish wine
c.   a small tree of the southeastern United States, also called sparkleberry

328. It's a bloomin' *bubby-bush,* all right!
(BUH-bee-bush)

a.   a red-flowered shrub found in the Carolinas
b.   a British policeman's hat
c.   truly a jolly good fellow

329. A wobbly *wickiup!*   *(WICK-ee-up)*

a.   a Fox and Kickapoo hut used by Indians in the southeastern United States
b.   an Australian pickup truck
c.   New England oil lamp

330. How about a *howdah* ride?   *(HOW-dah)*

a. a seat or covered pavilion on the back of an elephant or camel
b. a stagecoach with flat sides
c. a horse and buggy

331. Save the *spatterdock*.   *(SPAT-r-dok)*

a. a bathtub rubber duck
b. a seal's breathing hole in the ice
c. the common yellow water lily of eastern and central North America

332. Ride the *oont*.   *(UUNT)*

a. a horse (Arabia)
b. an elephant (India)
c. a camel (India)

333. Let's go cruising on the *nabby*.   *(NA-bee)*

a. an open sailboat with a lug rig and jib and a raking mast that is used especially for fishing off the eastern coast of Scotland
b. the float used by the British navy
c. a pirate ship

334. Check out the *chibouk*.   *(che-BUK)*

a. a tight rubber bandage for driving the blood out of a limb (German)
b. Eskimo term for an ice cream bar enclosed in a chocolate shell, often formed on a stick
c. a Turkish tobacco pipe having a clay or meerschaum bowl and a long stem, with a mouthpiece often of amber

335. I'll pass on *pantagamy*.   *(pan-TAG-a-mee)*

a. a communistic system of complex marriage, in which all the men and women of a household or community are regarded as married to one another
b. marriage in which the husband wears the pants, has all the authority
c. marriage in which the bride wears pants (slacks) at the wedding ceremony

336. Zero in on the *zalophus*.   *(ZAL-uh-fus)*

a. a genus of rather small-eared elephants (India)
b. a genus of rather small-eared seals, including the California sea dog
c. a genus of rather small-eared rabbits, including the cottontail (German)

337. A bellicose *bashi-bazouk.*
(BASH-ee-buh-ZOOK)

a. a conservative Republican
b. a liberal Democrat
c. a mercenary soldier belonging to the skirmishing or irregular troops of the Turkish army, notorious for their lawlessness, plundering, and brutality

338. That's *kismet.*   *(KIZ-met)*

a. fate (Turkish)
b. a loose curl falling across the forehead (Russian)
c. a West Atlantic language of the Kissi people

339. Let's play *able-whackets.*

a. ice hockey (Canada)
b. golf (Britain)
c. card game popular with sailors, wherein the loser is beaten over the palms of the hands with a handkerchief tightly twisted like a rope

340. She's down to her last *bawbee.*

a. a small Scottish coin
b. an Australian barbecue grill
c. the Japanese name for Barbie doll

341. A good *gillhooter*.   (gil-HOOT-r)

a.   a square-dance caller (American Ozarks)
b.   someone who tells whopper fish stories (Irish)
c.   owl, especially a barn owl (British)

342. It's like *love-in-a-mist*.

a.   perennial herb with small, fragrant, white flowers
b.   annual herb that does well in fog (Ireland)
c.   European garden plant having the flowers enveloped in numerous finely dissected bracts

343. Keep away from the *kaku*.   (KAH-ku)

a.   a great barracuda (Hawaiian)
b.   a sea monster (Norwegian legend)
c.   a deep ravine (South Africa)

344. Grip a *gambo*.   (GAM-bo)

a.   a viola (Africa)
b.   a farm cart used especially in Wales
c.   slang term for Gamblers Anonymous

345. Don't pick on the *pisonia*.

a.   an Italian cousin
b.   a small, bluish flower (Peru)
c.   a genus of tropical, often thorny, trees named after a Dutch physician and traveler

346. Put that in your *didgeridoo* and smoke it if you can.   *(DIJ-er-ee-DU)*

a.   a wooden pipe (Irish)
b.   a peace pipe (American Indians)
c.   a large musical pipe of the Australian aborigines made from bamboo

347. He's a daring *dike-louper*.

a.   a person who jumps dikes (Holland)
b.   a person who jumps fences (British)
c.   a person who jumps elephants (India)

348. Just what is a *jimswinger*?

a.   a long-tailed coat (southern and midland U.S.)
b.   a square dance (American Ozarks)
c.   a hammock (Brazil)

349. And just what is *jipijapa*?
(HEE-pee-HAH-pah)

a.   a barking dog (Mexico)
b.   a raw deal
c.   a Central and South American plant resembling a palm

350. There's a *bandy-bandy* in the grass.

a.   an Australian snake
b.   hanky-panky going on between lovers (Italy)
c.   A citizens band radio frequency scanner

351. What is a *kameel*?   (*ka-MEEL*)

a. giraffe (Africa)
b. fur from a camel used to make a kameel-hair coat
c. Vitamin K

352. What, pray tell, is a *kamik* made of? (*ka-MEEK*)

a. the saddle used on camels
b. an Eskimo sealskin boot
c. an Arabian bed, similar to the hammock, in which Bedouins sleep above hot, uncomfortable sand

353. What could *keddah* be?

a. Kurdish cheese made from goat's milk
b. an enclosure constructed to trap wild elephants (India)
c. a type of coffee bean grown in Colombia

354. What is *Kato*?   (*KAH-to*)

a. the special paddle used in a kayak
b. the mouthpiece of a musical instrument invented by Willem Kato
c. an Athapaskan people of northwestern California

355. Here comes the *love spoon*.

a. a wooden spoon, often with double bowl, formerly carved by a Welsh suitor as an engagement gift for his promised bride
b. a full moon
c. a wooden spoon used to tap the behind of toddlers for disciplinary reasons

356. He's seated on the *cutty stool*.

a. the stool used by cutlery repairmen or knife-sharpeners
b. a low stool; a seat in old Scottish churches where offenders, especially against chastity, were made to sit for public rebuke
c. the lookout seat on a sailing ship

357. Did you see that *daddynut?*

a. an oversized doughnut
b. American basswood
c. the main bolt holding the engine to an automobile chassis

358. I never saw a *dak runner* go so fast!

a. mail carrier (India and Burma)
b. blemish or tear in panty hose
c. Swedish long-distance runner

359. It's *niffy-naffy*.

a. a form or type of taffy
b. extremely important
c. trifling

360. That's really a *bumfreezer*.

a. a freezer that doesn't work
b. an oven
c. a boy's short jacket

361. What are the *Kickapoo*?

a. a Native American people originally of Wisconsin, now living in Oklahoma and Chihuahua, Mexico
b. missed field goals in a football game
c. meat dishes, similar to stew, served at gatherings in the Appalachian Mountains

362. Try traipsing around the *tidytips*.
(TI-dee-tips)

a. rows of tulips (Holland)
b. garden gloves and tools (British)
c. an annual California herb having yellow-rayed flower heads, often tipped in white

363. I love a good *chookie*.

a. a child (British)
b. a cookie (Australia)
c. a short, lofted golf stroke, used in approaching the green (Ireland)

364. A *keekwilee-house* is hard to get into!

a. a birdhouse for the kiwi
b. an Irish safe house for members of the IRA
c. an earth lodge partially below the surface of the ground, used by Indians of the northwestern coast of North America

365. That's a big *nordcaper*.   (*NORD-kap-r*)

a. a salad topping made of Norwegian capers
b. a Norwegian cap maker
c. a North Atlantic species of whale

366. Grab that *bonytail!*

a. a minnow of the Colorado River system that's rarely seen
b. a type of wild mustang found in the western U.S.
c. a French ponytail trimmed with ribbons or barrettes

367. You know, that's a *dunkadoo!*
(*DUN-ka-doo*)

a. any sugary Norwegian doughnut dipped in coffee
b. a shot in basketball when the ball completely misses the basket and backboard (Sweden)
c. American bittern or heron

368. I daresay, that's a *dumb betty*.

a. German slang for a not-too-bright waitress
b. a primitive mechanical household contrivance, such as a washing machine or dumbwaiter, used to lighten the workload of early American housewives
c. the automatic capper machine that caps bottles in an American beverage plant

369. *Bunji-bunji!*

a. South African dialect equivalent of the word "echo"
b. the rope carried and used by South American cattle workers or cowboys, made from the hair of horse tails
c. an Australian tree having bark that contains poison

370. Oil the skids with *dinkum oil*.

a. the forerunner of "snake oil" in the American West
b. oil from sperm whales used in manufacturing French perfumes
c. the truth (Australia)

371. Believe me, it's a *bobachee*.   *(BOB-a-chee)*

a. a female bobwhite
b. a male cook
c. a headache caused from bobbing for apples, an American custom at Halloween

372. What a *dinky-di*!

a. one who is loyal or true (Australia)
b. the eyelet of a ship's anchor, to which its chain or cable is attached
c. British for a very small sofa or divan

373. Bring out the *bubbly-jock*!   *(BUB-lee-jok)*

a. the clubhouse name for the winning jockey of the Kentucky Derby
b. champagne served at special British sports celebrations
c. a male turkey (Scottish)

374. What is a *zumbooruk*?   *(ZUM-bu-ruk)*

a. a wooden hut used by natives of the Zemburuk Mountains of New Guinea
b. a small cannon, mounted on a swivel, fired from a rest on the back of a camel
c. an African hammock

375. Have you ever seen a *zebu*?

a. an Asiatic ox
b. a male zebra
c. a newborn zebra colt

376. That's a *tattie doolie*, all right!

a. the New England lace edging 19th century table-cloths
b. the fringe that dangles from the sleeves of an American Indian jacket
c. a scarecrow in a potato field (Scottish)

377. A *ruby-and-topaz hummingbird* will give you a buzz.

a. a showy hummingbird of northern South America
b. a drink very popular in Argentina, made with red rum
c. what they call the Canadian equivalent of the Blue Angels flight team

378. No, that's not a rubber duck, but a *ruddy duck*.

a. English slang for the term "sailor"
b. a small boat powered by a small electric trolling motor in the Suez Canal
c. an American duck having a broad bill and a wedge-shaped tail

379. We've got here real *rumble gumption!*

a. good judgment, sense, intelligence (Scottish)
b. someone who fondly recalls an automobile with a rumble seat
c. street talk for a gang war

380. You'll find good, old-fashioned *timber doodle* just down the trail.

a. carvings on a tree such as hearts, initials, and dates
b. the American woodcock
c. flatbed truck trailer on which timber is hauled to saw mills, a term originating in Oregon

381. He was chafed by the *cheechako*.
(che-CHA-ko)

a. Eskimo moccasins made from sealskin
b. cold north wind blowing into Montana from Canada
c. tenderfoot in Alaska or the Pacific Northwest

382. We're facing *stoss*.

a. term for Spanish moss among Louisiana Cajuns
b. facing toward the direction from which an overriding glacier moves
c. the first assistant to a butler in a European manor house

383. *Wampum!*   *(WOM-pum)*

a. beads made of shells polished and strung together in strands, belts, and sashes, and used by North American Native Americans as money
b. a grass hut used by Native Americans in place of a tepee
c. bowl of an Indian ceremonial pipe filled with tobacco and smoked on special occasions

384. This is just a wee *spizella*.   *(spe-ZEL-ah)*

a. an Italian wine noted for its tangy aroma and taste
b. Sicilian spice from ground berries of the spizel bush
c. a genus of small American finches

385. Please, no *poorgirl*.

a. pigs and whistles (Scottish)
b. a southern U.S. reference to an unmarried girl
c. a po-boy or sub sandwich made only with vegetables (no meat)

386. Pick out the *pi-jaw*.

a. pious or moralizing talk
b. the marble used as a shooter in the game of marbles
c. the upper jaw, or palate

387. What is a *paniolo*?   *(PAN-ee-O-lo)*

a. an 18th century stringed musical instrument in Spain
b. the special cage in which panda bears are housed in a zoo
c. cowboy (Hawaii)

388. That's *kootcha*.   *(KU-chah)*

a. baby talk
b. a small, stingless wild Australian honeybee
c. the seat in an Eskimo kayak

389. Keep a good tie with your *neeper*.

a. a Scottish variation of "neighbor"
b. a type of clinging vine that grows wild in Europe
c. the small plastic end of a shoelace (Dutch)

390. Keep your distance from the *koodoo*.
(KOO-doo)

a. a South American jungle colt, similar to a roodoo
b. a large African antelope that has large, annulated, spirally twisted horns and is grayish brown with vertical white stripes on the sides
c. a very pungent cheese made from the milk of the yak

391. Anyone smell a *kokopu?*   *(KO-ke-pu)*

a. the hull or shell of the Brazilian cocoa bean
b. in the original Israeli kibbutzes, the outhouse
c. any of various New Zealand fishes that resemble the trout

392. You can almost hear the *kokako.* *(KO-ka-KO)*

a. a wattle crow (New Zealand)
b. a South American parrot
c. a Russian fur hat

393. Let's look at the *koolokamba.*

a. a native African dance
b. Sioux totem pole
c. a dark-faced West African chimpanzee, sometimes regarded as a separate species

394. Choose a king-size *koombar.*

a. an East Indian timber tree used especially for building foundations and for boat decks
b. a Pakistani treat resembling a chocolate cookie
c. a Korean musical instrument

395. A *koomkie* can run wild.

a. a wild flower resembling a violet that grows in Japanese mountains
b. a trained, usually female, elephant used in India to decoy and train wild male elephants
c. a type of glue or bonding agent used by plumbers

396. Go ahead—show your *Kuki-Chin.*
(KOO-kee-CHIN)

a. a group of Tibetan-Burmese languages spoken by the Kuki and Chin peoples
b. a Cary Grant chin, with a dimple or cleft
c. a type of Burmese carriage resembling the rickshaw, drawn or pulled by two men

397. A *penny-farthing* saved . . . would be worth a cat!

a. an English coin of the 17th century
b. a machine used by banks to roll large amounts of pennies
c. a bicycle with a large front wheel and a small rear wheel, common from about 1870 to 1890

398. Give me the *geta!*   *(GEH-ta)*

a. Japanese wooden clogs for outdoor wear
b. the Greek letter "G" (alpha, beta, delta, geta)
c. the symbol or scientific name for gamma ray

399. You can be penny-wise and pound-foolish with your *penysiller*.   *(PEN-nee-SILL-r)*

a. the paper wrapper around a roll of pennies
b. money, cash (Scottish)
c. a Scottish banker or company treasurer

400. Above all, entertain the *aikane*.
(i-KAYN-ee)

a. good friend (Hawaiian)
b. the French word for "icon"
c. something old and out-of-date

401. Ha! That's a real *kookaburra*!

a. spiny or thorny seeds from the Australian kooka tree
b. a kingfisher of Australia, about the size of a crow, that has a call resembling loud laughter and feeds in part on reptiles; called also "laughing jackass"
c. a native Colombian headdress

402. Were you awed by the *indaba*?
(in-DAB-ah)

a. the name of the great ape that raised Tarzan
b. a holy place or shrine in India
c. a conference, especially among representatives of South African tribes; party, talk

403. It seems the *ibex* vanished into the air.
(I-beks)

a. a computer database of information
b. one of several wild goats living chiefly in high mountain areas (as in the Alps)
c. a crane-like bird that summers in Holland

404. "Heads up" when it comes to a *hammam*.
(hah-MAHM)

a. an Oriental bathing establishment, a Turkish bath
b. a loin of pork
c. a footstool in India

405. Classified Ad: Now available, sharp-looking *betweenmaid*.

a. a domestic helper fired from one job and looking for another
b. a maidservant whose work supplements that of cook and housemaid
c. the black and white uniform of a housemaid

Index of
Answers

Answers appear alphabetically. The number of the question and the appropriate letter response (a, b, c, or d) are in parentheses following each word's correct definition.

abbey-lubber   a lazy monk **(26-b)**

able-whackets   a card game popular with sailors, wherein the loser is beaten over the palms of the hands with a handkerchief tightly twisted like a rope **(339-c)**

aglets   the metal coverings at the ends of shoelaces **(12-a)**

agrostographer   a writer whose subject is grass **(97-a)**

aide-de-camp   a military aide **(200-c)**

aikane   good friend (Hawaiian) **(400-a)**

aileron   a flight maneuver in which an airplane rotates about its longitudinal axis through a full 360 degrees (by means of *ailerons*) without altering its flight path **(201-b)**

amoret   a sweetheart; an amorous girl **(102-c)**

aubade   a song greeting the dawn **(82-b)**

auspice   observation, especially of the flight and feeding of birds, intended to discover a sign of the future **(123-c)**

badderlocks   a large, brownish black seaweed often eaten as a vegetable in Europe **(227-b)**

baggywrinkles   a frayed rope on a ship **(1-c)**

baked Alaska   a dessert consisting of cake topped with ice cream covered with meringue and quickly browned in an oven **(257-c)**

baksheesh   a tip; gratuity **(111-b)**

balabosta   an efficient Jewish housewife **(44-a)**

ballahoo   a schooner of Bermuda and the West Indies with its foremast raking forward and its main staff aft **(280-c)**

ballhooter   a logger who rolls logs down slopes too steep for teams of horses **(135-c)**

ballyhoo   an attention-getting demonstration or talk, as by a barker **(289-c)**

Banbury tart   an often triangular tart with a fruit filling, especially of raisins, from Banbury, England **(238-c)**

bandy-bandy   an Australian snake **(350-a)**

bashi-bazouk   a mercenary soldier belonging to the skirmishing or irregular troops of the Turkish army, notorious for their lawlessness, plundering, and brutality **(337-c)**

bathbun   a round bun made of sweet yeast dough containing eggs, butter, and currants **(221-c)**

bawbee   a small Scottish coin **(340-a)**

beanfest   a noisy good time (British) **(304-c)**

bee louse   a minute wingless fly parasitic on honeybees **(125-a)**

beenamarriage   a marriage in parts of India and Ceylon in which the husband enters the wife's kinship group and has little authority in the household **(324-c)**

beer and skittles   drink and play; easy-going enjoyment **(303-b)**

belladonna   a poisonous Eurasian plant having purplish red, bell-shaped flowers **(41-b)**

bellicose   warlike, aggressive, combative **(156-b)**

belltopper   a tall silk hat (Australian) **(124-c)**

belly robber   a cook; steward **(248-a)**

beturbaned   one who is wearing a turban **(208-c)**

betwattled   addled, confused **(207-b)**

betweenmaid   a maidservant whose work supplements that of cook and housemaid **(405-b)**

bib nozzle   a bent-down nozzle of a faucet often threaded for attachment of a hose **(210-c)**

bibliophile   a lover of books, especially beautiful or rare books with unusual formats **(212-a)**

bibliotaph   a person who hides or hoards books **(213-b)**

billywix   a tawny owl **(110-c)**

birdie   to shoot a hole in golf in one stroke under par **(278-a)**

biscuit shooter   a cook or waiter especially in a camp or on a ranch **(237-b)**

bittock   a little bit (Scottish) **(163-b)**

blithemeat   food prepared for a feast to celebrate the birth of a child (Scottish) **(298-b)**

blizzard head   a woman television performer with hair so blonde that special lighting is required to prevent a flare or halo from appearing on screen. **(47-c)**

blotto   completely drunk **(297-c)**

blue devils   low spirits, melancholy **(164-a)**

bobachee   a male cook **(371-b)**

bobadill   a cowardly braggart **(131-c)**

bonnyclabber   thick sour milk **(225-b)**

bonytail   a minnow of the Colorado River system that's rarely seen **(366-a)**

boodle   estate and property **(15-a)**

borborygmus   a growling intestine (time to eat!) **(37-b)**

bowwow theory   a theory that language originated in imitations of natural sounds, such as those of birds, dogs, or thunder **(197-c)**

bubblet   a small bubble **(299-c)**

bubbly-jock   a male turkey (Scottish) **(373-c)**

bubby-bush   a red-flowered shrub found in the Carolinas **(328-a)**

bumble-puppy   an old game resembling bagatelle, but played outdoors with marbles **(292-b)**

bumblekite   a belief that blackberries cause flatulence **(13-b)**

bumfreezer   a boy's short jacket **(360-c)**

bumfuzzled   confused, perplexed, flustered **(126-b)**

bungtowns   copper tokens resembling English halfpennies that circulated in the U.S. in the 18th and 19th centuries **(116-c)**

bunji-bunji   an Australian tree having bark that contains poison **(369-c)**

bunny hug   an American ballroom dance in ragtime rhythm, popular in the early 20th century, in which a couple holds each other closely **(132-a)**

burgoo   a thick oatmeal gruel used chiefly by seamen **(133-c)**

buttercup squash   a turban squash with flesh resembling a sweet potato in flavor **(258-c)**

cacography   bad writing, bad handwriting **(122-b)**

calaboose   jail **(157-c)**

calipash   the fatty, gelatinous, dull-green substance found under the upper shell of a turtle that's esteemed as a delicacy **(96-a)**

callipygian   having a shapely bottom (buttocks) **(66-a)**

canoodle   to cuddle amorously **(84-a)**

cattalo   a hybrid of the American buffalo and the domestic cow **(85-b)**

celerity   swiftness, speed **(53-c)**

checkerbelly   a white-fronted goose **(108-c)**

cheechako   a tenderfoot in Alaska or the Pacific Northwest **(381-c)**

chibouk   a Turkish tobacco pipe having a clay or meer-schaum bowl and a long stem, with a mouthpiece often of amber **(334-c)**

chicha   a South and Central American beer made from fermented maize **(95-a)**

chookie   a child (British) **(363-a)**

chuffy   fat, chubby **(155-b)**

claro   a light-colored, generally mild cigar **(154-c)**

climax basket   a small, oblong, veneer basket with rounded ends **(306-a)**

cock ale   ale fermented with fruits, spices, and the jelly or mincemeat of a boiled cock **(260-a)**

cock-a-hoop   to live extravagantly **(290-a)**

cock-a-leekie   a soup made of chicken boiled with leeks **(259-b)**

cockarouse   a person of consequence among the American colonists **(25-b)**

cockshut   evening twilight **(80-a)**

contrabass   largest instrument of the viol family **(87-a)**

coolamon   an Australian vessel of bark or wood that resembles a basin and is used for carrying and holding water **(307-a)**

cowfish   any of various small cetaceans, such as the grampus and some species of porpoise and dolphin **(158-c)**

coxcomb   a jester's cap worn by a professional fool **(94-c)**

crambo   a game in which one player gives a word or line of a verse that's matched in rhyme by other players **(291-a)**

criticaster   an inferior critic **(23-a)**

cuckoo-button   a prickly burr **(11-a)**

cutty stool   a low stool; a seat in old Scottish churches where offenders, especially against chastity, were made to sit for public rebuke **(356-b)**

cuttyhunk   a hand-laid twisted linen fishing line suitable for deep-sea sport fishing **(279-b)**

daddynut   American basswood **(357-b)**

dak runner   mail carrier (India and Burma) **(358-a)**

dandiprat   an English silver coin of the 16th century probably worth twopence **(98-c)**

dibble   a small hand instrument used to make holes in the ground for plants **(34-c)**

diddle daddle   fuss **(113-c)**

diddledees   fallen pine needles **(117-a)**

didgeridoo   a large musical pipe of the Australian aborigines made from bamboo **(346-c)**

dike-louper   a person who jumps fences (British) **(347-b)**

dingbat   a typographical ornament (as a bullet or star) used typically to call attention to an opening sentence **(134-b)**

dingdong theory   a theory that language originated from a natural correspondence between objects of sense perception and the vocal noises which were part of early humans' reaction to them (whew!) **(119-c)**

dinkum oil   the truth (Australia) **(370-c)**

dinky-di   one who is loyal or true (Australia) **(372-a)**

dipsy doodle   a bewildering plunge and lag by turns **(63-c)**

dockwalloper   a loafer about docks who picks up casual employment **(271-b)**

dog cabbage   a fleshy southern European herb often eaten as a potherb **(244-d)**

doodlesack   a bagpipe **(325-b)**

dooteroomus   money **(40-c)**

draggle-tail   a woman who lets her skirt trail along the ground **(140-c)**

dragoman   an interpreter chiefly of Arabic, Turkish, or Persian employed as official interpreter by an embassy or as a guide by tourists **(318-b)**

dumb betty   a primitive mechanical household contrivance, such as a washing machine or dumbwaiter, used to lighten the workload of early American housewives **(368-b)**

dunkadoo   American bittern or heron **(367-c)**

echolalia   the often pathological repetition of what is said by other people as if echoing them **(216-c)**

fair dinkum   unquestionably good or genuine; excellent—often used as a general expression of approval (Australian) **(147-a)**

fairy butter   a blue-green algae, forming gelatinous sheets or pellets **(148-b)**

farkleberry   a small tree of the southeastern United States, also called sparkleberry **(327-c)**

farthingale   a hooped petticoat worn in the 16th century **(42-a)**

fimble   the male hemp plant that produces a weaker and shorter fiber than the female plant **(127-c)**

fipple   a grooved plug in the end of a whistle **(272-c)**

flamdoodle   a line of pretentious nonsense **(146-c)**

flews   the large chaps (hanging upper lips) of a deep-mouthed hound, like a bloodhound **(71-a)**

flicker-a-flacket   a representation of the sound made by something flapping **(121-c)**

foozle   to play unskillfully; to bungle **(288-a)**

gambo a farm cart used especially in Wales **(344-b)**

gamp slang for umbrella **(138-a)**

gardyloo a warning shout in Scotland when it was customary to throw household slops from upstairs windows: "Attention to the water!" **(73-c)**

gazook a guy **(35-b)**

gazoz a carbonated nonalcoholic drink **(261-c)**

gedunk something (like a sundae) sold at a soda fountain or snack bar **(276-c)**

gee-throw a strong wooden lever with a curved metal point used to break out logging sleds **(191-c)**

geta Japanese wooden clogs for outdoor wear **(398-a)**

gill-go-by-the-ground a ground ivy **(76-c)**

gillaroo an Irish trout **(229-a)**

gillflirt a giddy or shameless girl **(75-a)**

gillhooter owl, especially a barn owl (British) **(341-c)**

gimcrackery a collection of flimsy doodads, chegans, or trifles **(226-c)**

googol the figure "1" followed by a hundred zeros **(22-a)**

gopher ball a pitched ball hit for extra bases, specifically one hit for a home run **(284-c)**

gorp a healthy mixture of dried fruit, nuts, and seeds **(222-a)**

graphospasm a writer's cramp **(55-a)**

griggles small or inferior apples remaining on a tree after harvest **(39-a)**

guitarfish any of several viviparous rays of the family rhinobatidae somewhat resembling a guitar in outline when viewed from above **(286-a)**

gumshoe a detective **(6-b)**

gustation the sensation of tasting **(219-c)**

halieutics the art of fishing **(287-a)**

hammam an Oriental bathing establishment, a Turkish bath **(404-a)**

heliophiles people attracted to sunlight **(294-a)**

hippocras a spice-flavored wine **(269-c)**

hoddy-doddy   a garden snail **(192-b)**

hoddypoll   a fumbling, inept person **(193-a)**

hoecake   a small cake made of cornmeal, water, and salt, so named from its being baked on the blade of a hoe **(262-b)**

holus-bobus   all in a lump, all together **(78-b)**

honeycreeper   a small brightly colored oscine bird of the Coerebridge family found in tropical and subtropical America **(64-b)**

honeypot   a receptacle for storing honey **(223-b)**

hornswoggle   a bamboozle, a hoax **(27-a)**

horripilation   goosebumps **(57-a)**

hotsy-totsy   comfortably stable or secure **(141-b)**

howdah   a seat or covered pavilion on the back of an elephant or camel **(330-a)**

howdie   midwife **(106-a)**

hubble-bubble   a water pipe **(149-a)**

huckaback   a tough, durable type of cotton **(150-c)**

hug-me-tight   a woman's short, close-fitting bed jacket **(56-a)**

hugger-mugger   an act of secrecy and concealment **(9-a)**

ibex   one of several wild goats living chiefly in high mountain areas (as in the Alps) **(403-b)**

indaba   a conference, especially among representatives of South African tribes; party, talk **(402-c)**

infradig   beneath one's dignity **(209-b)**

inglenook   a corner by the fire **(83-a)**

inky-cap   a mushroom **(218-b)**

inquiline   an animal that lives habitually in the nest or abode of some other species **(168-c)**

jabiru   a large stork of tropical America **(72-a)**

jack-a-dandy   a little, foppish impertinent fellow **(153-b)**

jack-in-office   an insolent fellow in authority **(152-c)**

jack-pudding buffoon   a clown **(300-a)**

jackalegs   a large clasp knife (Scottish) **(247-c)**

jelly roll   a thin sheet of sponge cake spread with jelly and rolled up while hot **(242-c)**

jigger pump   a pump to force beer into vats **(246-d)**

jiggery-pokery   humbug, nonsense (British) **(159-a)**

Jim Hill mustard   tumble mustard named after James J. Hill **(245-a)**

jimjams   delirium tremens; also overwrought from excess or fear **(151-b)**

jimswinger   a long-tailed coat (South and midland U.S.) **(348-a)**

jingbang   crowd, company **(89-b)**

jinglet   the bell clapper of a sleigh bell **(301-c)**

jingo ring   a singing game in which children join hands and dance around one child in the center **(305-b)**

jipijapa   a Central and South American plant resembling a palm **(349-c)**

jokelet   a little joke **(302-a)**

jumbuck   a sheep native to Australia **(58-a)**

justaucorps   a man's close-fitting, knee-length garment; a body coat **(128-a)**

kaka   New Zealand parrot that talks and mimics well **(315-a)**

kaku   a great barracuda (Hawaiian) **(343-a)**

kameel   giraffe (Africa) **(351-a)**

kamik   an Eskimo sealskin boot **(352-b)**

Kato   an Athapaskan people of northwestern California **(354-c)**

katzenjammer   a hangover—the nausea, headache, and debility following drunkenness. **(69-c)**

keddah   An enclosure constructed to trap wild elephants (India) **(353-b)**

keekwilee-house   an earth lodge partially below the surface of the ground used by Native American people of the northwestern coast of North America **(364-c)**

kef   a state of dreamy tranquility **(202-a)**

kelpie   an Australian inner tube made of kelp **(180-a)**

kenspeckled   Scottish word meaning conspicuous, having a distinct appearance **(18-b)**

kerfuffle   a commotion, fuss **(17-b)**

Kickapoo   a Native American people originally of Wisconsin but now living in Oklahoma and Chihuahua, Mexico **(361-a)**

kickshaw   a fancy dish in cookery **(54-a)**

kidcote   jail **(112-a)**

kielbasa   uncooked smoked sausage **(236-d)**

king plank   the center plank of a wooden deck **(190-a)**

kinkcough   whooping cough **(107-c)**

kismet   fate (Turkish) **(338-a)**

kiss-in-the-ring   the game drop-the-handkerchief, in which the pursuing player may kiss the player he catches **(310-b)**

kiss-me-over-the-garden-gate   a plant **(203-a)**

kiss-me-quick   a small bonnet worn off the face, especially in the latter half of the 19th century **(204-c)**

kissing gate   a gate swinging in a V-shaped enclosure that allows only one person to pass at a time **(206-c)**

kittenball   softball **(277-c)**

kittle cattle   a group of people difficult to manage and inclined to be capricious **(142-c)**

kittly-benders   thin, bending ice **(88-c)**

klapmatch   a female seal **(74-a)**

knuckle-duster   brass knuckles **(283-b)**

koh-i-noor   something thought to be the best of its kind, especially an usually large and valuable diamond **(205-a)**

kokako   a wattle crow (New Zealand) **(392-a)**

kokopu   any of various New Zealand fishes that resemble the trout **(391-c)**

koodoo   a large African antelope that has large, annulated, spirally twisted horns and is grayish brown with vertical white stripes on the sides **(390-b)**

kookaburra   a kingfisher of Australia, about the size of a crow, that has a call resembling loud laughter and feeds in part on reptiles; called also "laughing jackass" **(401-b)**

koolokamba   a dark-faced West African chimpanzee sometimes regarded as a separate species **(393-c)**

koombar   an East Indian timber tree used especially for building foundations and for boat decks **(394-a)**

koomkie a trained, usually female, elephant used in India to decoy and train wild male elephants **(395-b)**

kootcha a small, stingless, wild Australian honeybee **(388-b)**

Kuki-Chin a group of Tibetan-Burmese languages spoken by the Kuki and Chin peoples **(396-a)**

kumara a sweet potato (New Zealand) **(252-c)**

ladykin a little lady, sometimes used as an endearment **(77-b)**

lagniappe a small gift given a customer by a merchant at the time of a purchase **(59-c)**

lalapalooza an excellent person or thing; a humdinger **(16-a)**

lickerish a person fond of fine food **(228-c)**

lip-deep plunged in to the lips (no deeper than the lips) **(184-a)**

liripoop a tassel that hangs over a graduate's hat **(5-b)**

loco foco a match or cigar developed during the 19th century that's capable of being ignited by friction on any hard, dry, rough surface **(103-b)**

logomach one who fights about words **(28-a)**

love apple tomato **(233-c)**

love spoon a wooden spoon often with double bowl, formerly carved by a Welsh suitor as an engagement gift for his promised bride **(355-a)**

love-in-a-mist European garden plant having the flowers enveloped in numerous finely dissected bracts **(342-c)**

mashie niblick an old golf club, also called a six iron **(270-a)**

melophagus a genus of wingless flies **(183-b)**

milk punch a mixed drink of alcoholic liquor, milk, and sugar **(234-d)**

Minié ball a rifle bullet having a cylindrical body, conical head, and hollow base, much used in the mid-19th century **(285-b)**

moll-buzzer   a pickpocket whose victims are women **(194-c)**

molly-coddle   a pampered darling; a spineless weakling **(195-b)**

nabby   an open sailboat with a lug rig and jib and a raking mast that is used especially for fishing off the eastern coast of Scotland **(333-a)**

Nantucket sleighride   a run in a whaling boat to a harpooned whale **(198-b)**

napfkuchen   a semisweet cake (German) **(224-c)**

napoo   British slang used to indicate that something is finished, incapacitated, dead, all gone, or nonexistent, or that the answer is "no" **(186-a)**

naricorn   a horny covering protecting the nostrils of certain birds **(185-b)**

neeper   a Scottish variation of "neighbor" **(389-a)**

neffy   variation of "nephew" **(181-a)**

nehu   a small Hawaiian anchovy much used for bait **(253-a)**

nid-nod   to nod repeatedly from drowsiness **(214-a)**

niddicock   a fool, a ninny **(130-c)**

niddle-noodle   an unstable nodding head **(109-a)**

niddle   to move quickly **(129-c)**

niddy-noddy   a hand reel for yarn **(29-c)**

niffy-naffy   trifling **(359-c)**

nipa   an alcoholic beverage made from the fermented sap of an Australian palm **(239-d)**

nipperkin   a container that holds a half-pint of hooch **(31-a)**

noctambulist   one who walks at night, especially in his sleep **(187-c)**

nodding catchfly   a perennial European sticky herb **(241-a)**

nodding onion   a widely distributed North American bulbous herb with white to deep rose flowers, also called a wild onion **(240-b)**

nordcaper   a North Atlantic species of whale **(365-c)**

nuddle   to push with the nose, often close to the ground;

to grovel **(60-b)**

oenotherapy   the use of wine for therapeutic purposes **(65-a)**

okapi   a giraffe-like animal with a short neck and black-and-white-striped upper legs **(45-a)**

oleaster   a wild olive tree **(220-a)**

oont   a camel (India) **(332-c)**

oopak   any of several black teas grown in Hupeh province of China **(254-b)**

Oregon boot   a heavy iron shackle attached to the ankle and foot of a prisoner to prevent escape **(170-a)**

oscitate   to yawn **(188-a)**

osculate   kiss **(10-a)**

oxymoron   a phrase that contradicts itself (i.e., a "quiet explosion") **(8-a)**

palooka   an inexperienced or incompetent boxer **(282-c)**

paniolo   cowboy (Hawaii) **(387-c)**

pannikin   a small cup or pan, often of tin **(217-c)**

pansophist   a know-it-all **(38-a)**

pantagamy   marriage practiced in some communist societies in which every man is regarded as the husband and every woman a wife in a kind of group marriage **(335-a)**

pantofle   a bedroom slipper. **(52-a)**

paradiddle   a military marching drum beat **(7-a)**

paradoctor   a doctor who reaches isolated areas by parachute **(145-a)**

paranut   Brazil nut **(232-a)**

pea goose   a poor simpleton; ninny **(139-a)**

pease porridge   pea soup **(199-b)**

pelmatogram   an impression of the sole of the foot **(189-c)**

pennywinkle   a periwinkle **(144-b)**

penny-farthing   a bicycle with a large front wheel and a small rear wheel, common from about 1870 to 1890 **(397-c)**

pennyprick   an old game of aiming at a penny **(309-a)**

pennysiller   money; cash (Scottish) **(399-b)**

penster   a writer (**92-c**)

perwitsky   a red, white, and black European tiger weasel (**323-b**)

pettifogger   a rascally attorney (**2-c**)

philodox   a person who just loves his own opinion (**32-b**)

pi-jaw   pious or moralizing talk (**386-a**)

pickelhaube   a spiked helmet worn by German soldiers (**3-c**)

picotee   a flower (as carnation, tulip, rose) having one basic color with a margin of another color (**182-c**)

pigs in blankets   oysters, chicken livers, or other choice morsels wrapped in thin slices of bacon, fastened with skewers, and broiled or sauteed (**250-a**)

pigwidgeon   an insignificant or simple person (**178-a**)

pill masser   a machine that mixes ingredients for pills (**176-c**)

pilliwinks   an old instrument of torture for the thumbs and fingers (**175-a**)

pillowbeer   a pillowcase (**177-b**)

pip-pip   "So long!" "Good-bye!" (**326-c**)

pishpash   a rice broth containing bits of meat (**251-d**)

pisonia   a genus of tropical, often thorny, trees named after a Dutch physician and traveler (**345-c**)

polyglot   a person who speaks or writes several languages (**215-b**)

ponhaws   a dish of leftovers, scrapple (**268-a**)

poo-bah   one holding many public or private offices (**100-b**)

pooh-pooh theory   a theory that language originated in interjections which gradually acquired meaning (**118-a**)

pook   heaps or small stacks of hay or grain (**101-a**)

poonac   coconut cake (**235-a**)

poorgirl   pigs and whistles (Scottish) (**385-a**)

Popocrat   a Democrat supporting Populist policies in the last decade of the 19th century, usually used disparagingly (**173-a**)

popinjay a parrot **(211-b)**

pother a noisy disturbance, bustle **(50-b)**

pottle a liquid or dry measure equal to a half-gallon **(172-c)**

pretty-by-night four o'clock **(137-b)**

prickmedainty affectedly nice; goody-goody **(99-b)**

prosit a toast used to wish good health, especially before drinking **(308-c)**

quaddle a person who grumbles **(51-a)**

quadragenarian anyone between forty and fifty years old **(19-a)**

quahog a thick-shelled American clam **(79-c)**

quark croak **(166-c)**

quarson a clergyman who also holds the position of squire in his parish **(179-a)**

quiddity a hairsplitting distinction **(167-a)**

quidnunc a busybody, newsmonger, gossip **(46-a)**

rarebit Welsh rabbit; melted and often seasoned cheese sometimes mixed with ale or beer and poured over toasted bread or crackers **(255-a)**

ruby-and-topaz hummingbird a showy hummingbird of northern South America **(377-a)**

ruddy duck an American duck having a broad bill and a wedge-shaped tail **(378-c)**

rudesby an uncivil, turbulent person **(174-c)**

rumble gumption good judgment, sense, intelligence (Scottish) **(379-a)**

samlet a young salmon **(265-c)**

scapegrace a reckless, unprincipled person **(62-b)**

scaramouch a stock character in the Italian commedia dell'arte **(14-c)**

schmooze chat **(293-a)**

shepherd's pie a savory mixture of leftover meat baked in a crust of mashed potatoes **(256-c)**

shilly-shally vacillate and be undecided **(4-c)**

siffleur a whistler **(161-b)**

simoleon   dollar **(317-a)**

sine die   indefinitely, without any future date designated to resume business **(160-c)**

singlet   an undershirt or athletic jersey **(61-b)**

singultus   hiccups **(70-a)**

sippet   a small bit or piece of toast soaked in milk or broth **(266-d)**

slumgullion   an insipid drink, such as weak tea or coffee **(263-c)**

smicket   a woman's smock (English) **(114-c)**

snippersnapper   whippersnapper **(105-c)**

snoozle   to cuddle, snuggle **(104-a)**

spanker boom   the boom for a spanker on a ship **(162-c)**

spatterdock   the common yellow water lily of eastern and central North America **(331-c)**

spelunker   someone who explores caves **(274-a)**

spizella   a genus of small American finches **(384-c)**

spizzerinctum   the will to succeed; vim, energy, ambition **(273-a)**

splacknuck   an unusual animal mentioned by Jonathan Swift in *Gulliver's Travels* **(24-c)**

squirting cucumber   a Mediterranean plant having oblong fruit that bursts from the peduncle when ripe and forcibly ejects its seeds **(264-a)**

stoss   facing toward the direction from which an overriding glacier moves **(382-b)**

stumblebum   a punch-drunk, clumsy, or inept boxer **(281-a)**

swell mob   a group of criminals who dress fashionably and act with seeming respectability **(169-c)**

swillbowl   a drunkard **(295-a)**

syllabub   a drink or dessert made by curdling milk or cream with wine or other acid **(267-c)**

taradiddle   the fib **(21-a)**

tarantism   a dancing mania caused by the bite of a tarantula **(165-b)**

tattie doolie   a scarecrow in a potato field (Scottish) **(376-c)**
tidytips   an annual California herb having yellow-rayed flower heads often tipped in white **(362-c)**
tim-whiskey   whiskey **(243-a)**
timber doodle   the American woodcock **(380-b)**
Tin Lizzie   a nickname for the Model T Ford automobile **(91-a)**
tinker's damn   something absolutely worthless **(90-c)**
tipsy pudding   stale sponge cake soaked in wine, especially sherry, and served with custard **(231-c)**
titi   a South American monkey **(316-b)**
toad-in-the-hole meat   meat (as sausage) cooked in batter usually by baking **(230-c)**
toby   a small jug, pitcher, or mug generally used for ale and shaped like a stout man with a cocked hat **(296-c)**
tonga   a light two-wheeled vehicle for two or four persons drawn by one horse and common in India **(314-b)**
twit-twat   the switch or handle that controls the speed of a diesel engine **(143-b)**
tzut   a brightly patterned square of cotton used by Guatemalans, especially as a head cover **(321-c)**
uxorious   doting on, with excessive fondness for, and often submissive to, a wife **(68-c)**
vamper   a stocking **(115-a)**
view halloo   a shout uttered by a hunter on seeing a fox break cover **(275-a)**
wainwright   one who builds and repairs wagons **(36-c)**
wampum   beads made of shells polished and strung together in strands, belts, and sashes, and used by the North American Native Americans as money **(383-a)**
wayzgoose   a printer's annual outing or entertainment **(171-a)**
whiffle   something light or insignificant, a trifle **(49-a)**
whippet   a small dog **(43-a)**
wickiup   a Fox and Kickapoo hut used by Indians in the southeastern United States **(329-a)**

wiki wiki   a Hawaiian adverb meaning quickly; fast **(313-c)**
williwaw   a sudden, violent gust of cold air **(20-a)**
willy-nilly   "whether you like it or not" **(33-c)**
wonga wonga   an Australian woody vine with loose panicles of yellowish white flowers **(312-a)**
wonky   unsteady, shaky **(30-c)**
woodmonger   a dealer in wood; a timber merchant **(93-a)**
wooly bear   a very large caterpillar **(86-c)**
yaffle   a green woodpecker that makes a laughing sound **(48-a)**
yeti   Abominable Snowman **(196-b)**
yokefellow   a close associate or companion; a partner in marriage **(67-b)**
younker   a young man; child, youngster **(81-c)**
zalophus   a genus of rather small-eared seals, including the California sea dog **(336-b)**
zap flap   an airplane wing flap **(311-a)**
zarf   a cup-shaped holder for a hot coffee cup used in the Levant, usually of metal and of ornamental design **(320-a)**
zebu   an Asiatic ox **(375-a)**
ziggurat   an ancient Babylonian temple **(322-a)**
zimb   a large two-winged fly native to Abyssinia **(319-a)**
Zingaro   the Italian name for Gypsy, Rom **(120-a)**
zooty   extreme or flashy in manner or style **(136-c)**
zumbooruk   a small cannon, mounted on a swivel, fired from a rest on the back of a camel **(374-b)**